SECRETS FROM A WANDERING SOUL
PART I
BY ALICE HARMON

(C) 2017 ALICE HARMON.
ALL RIGHTS RESERVED.

CHAPTER ONE
WHISPERS

CHAPTER TWO
AURA

CHAPTER THREE
VIBRATIONS

CHAPTER FOUR
CONNECTED

CHAPTER ONE

WHISPERS

you are
the summation
of all the potential
for good things
in the universe

i want to touch
the river
that bathed humanity
in the light of life

fear
is the most dangerous thing
you can let
into your mind

tell me

if you could travel
anywhere in the world

where would you go?
what would you do?

now tell me...
what's stopping you?

if i waited
on the bench
where i first met you

how long would it take you
to come looking for me?

how long would it take
for your soul
to lead you back
to mine?

always choose
to speak life
into the lives
of those around you

you never know
when they'll need it most

how can i be
in a city
of a million people

and yet
still feel

a l o n e ?

hidden among
this concrete jungle
are a thousand
beautiful stories
of love and loss
life and death

in this broken system
humanity
is herded like cattle
to and fro
doing
what their corporate masters
dictate

we were meant
for so much more
than working
and dying.

there is something so beautiful
about sharing in the talents
of strangers

watching them grow
and develop
contributing
to our world

the universe
did not conspire
to create you
from planets and stardust
so you could live a life
of chasing after
material things

a hand to hold
against the cold

nothing could be
so beautiful as this

two souls
connected by fingertips
as electricity
flows between us

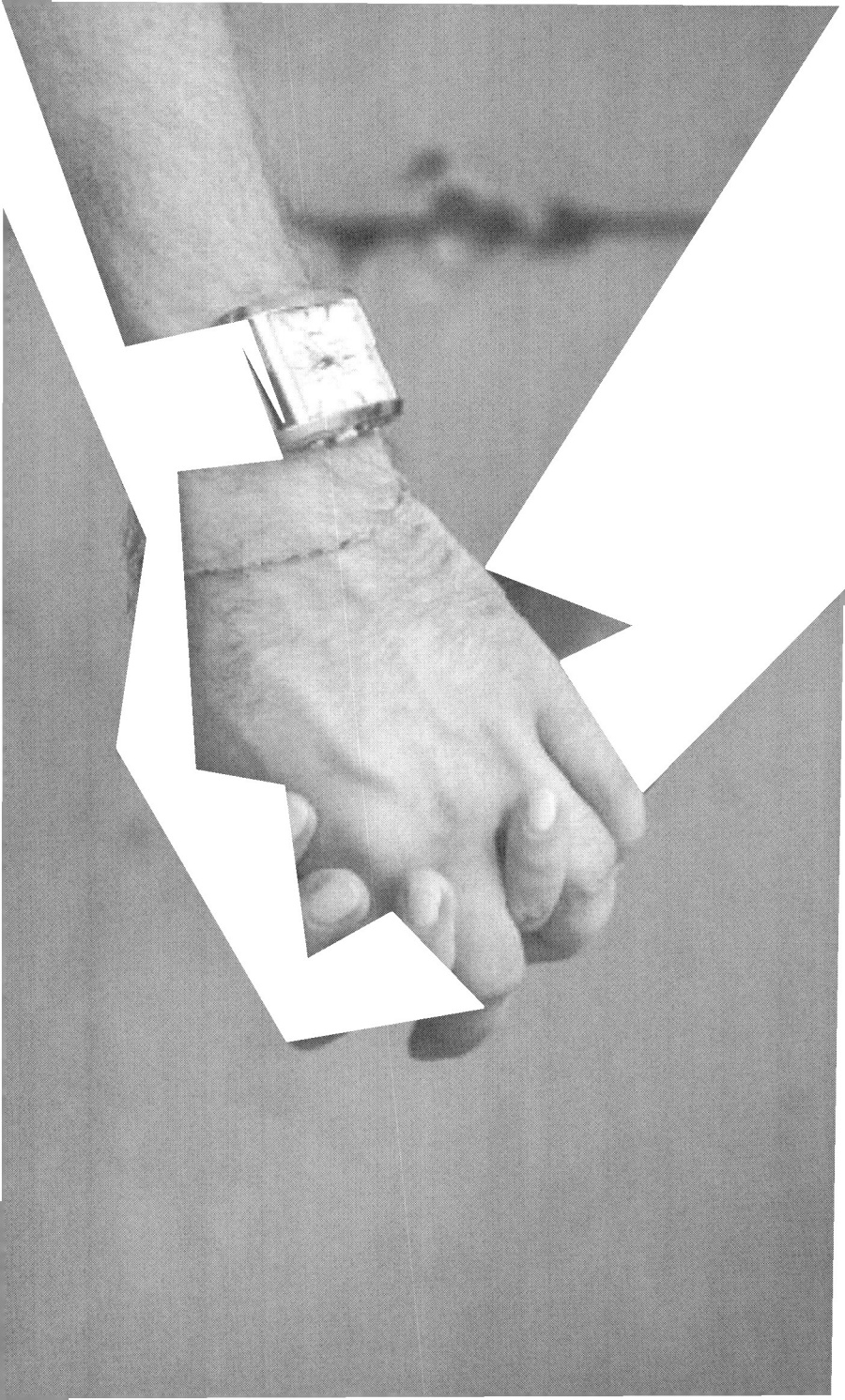

i walk alone
through this crowded city
wondering
where my path leads
and where destiny
will lead me

CHAPTER TWO

AURA

seven billion people
jostling for power
all seeking
to be at the top
of this
grotesque pyramid
we've made ourselves into

take time
for yourself
today.

pour yourself
some coffee

think about
your life

are you happy?
if not,
how can you make
yourself happy?

this is what i want
for you
today.

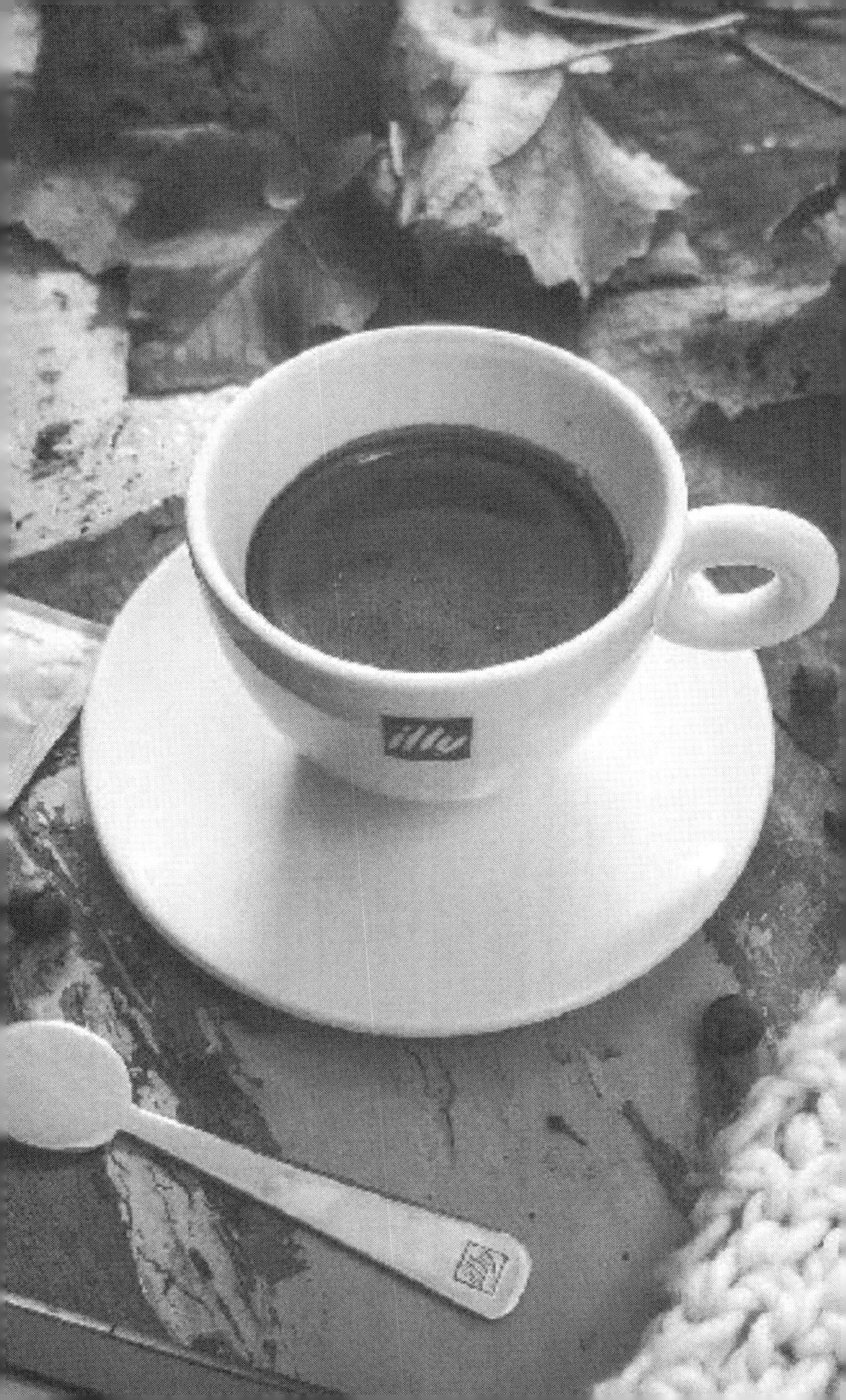

i admit
that even i
am sometimes confused
by the way life goes

but that's alright.

everything will work out
for good
in the end.

he took me
to the ocean
and told me

darling,
let us sail together
on an ocean
of all the tears
we have ever wept
over people
who weren't right
for us

let us sail together,
you and i
and never come back...

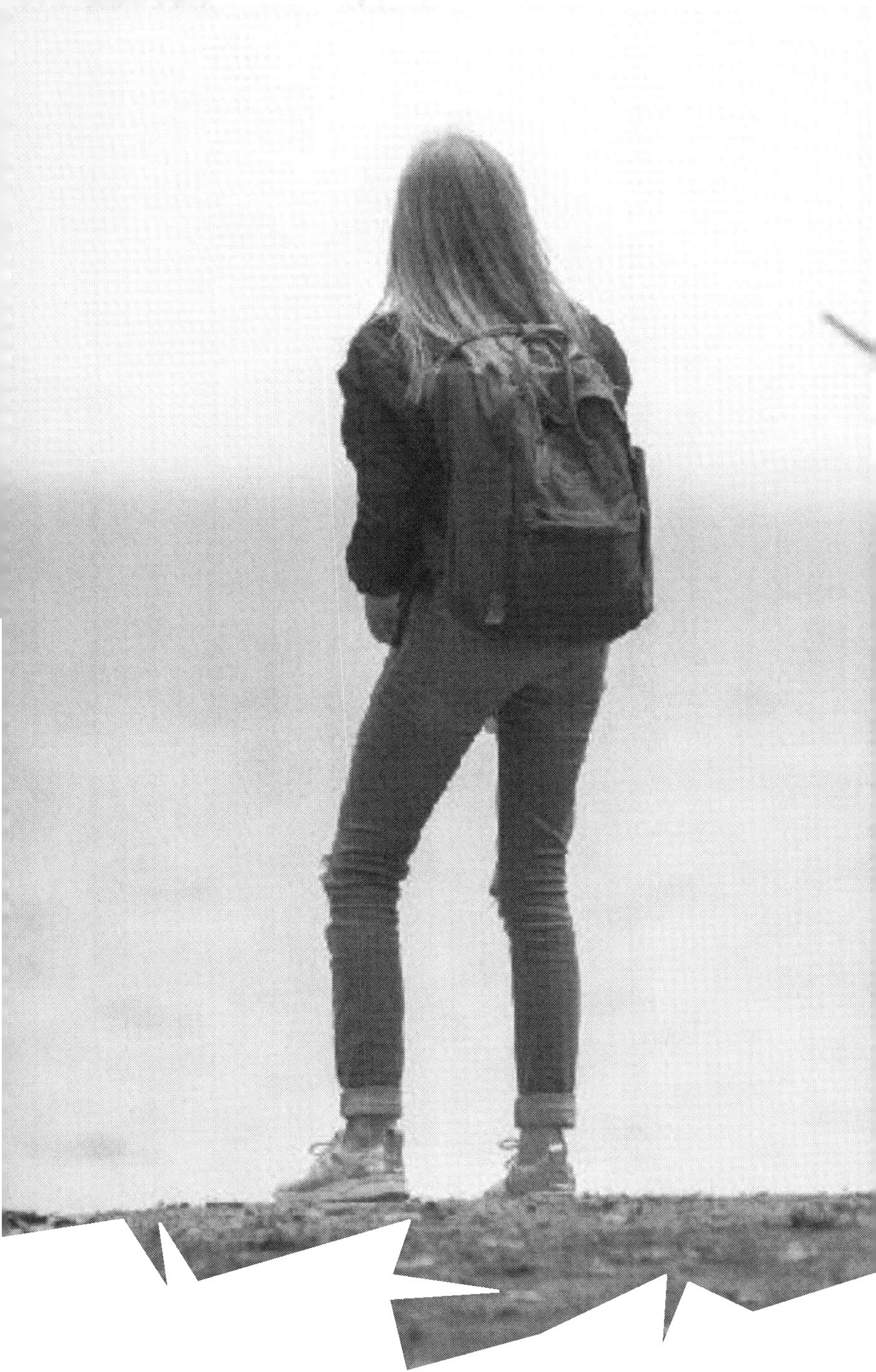

the leaves may change
with the seasons
but my feelings for you
never will

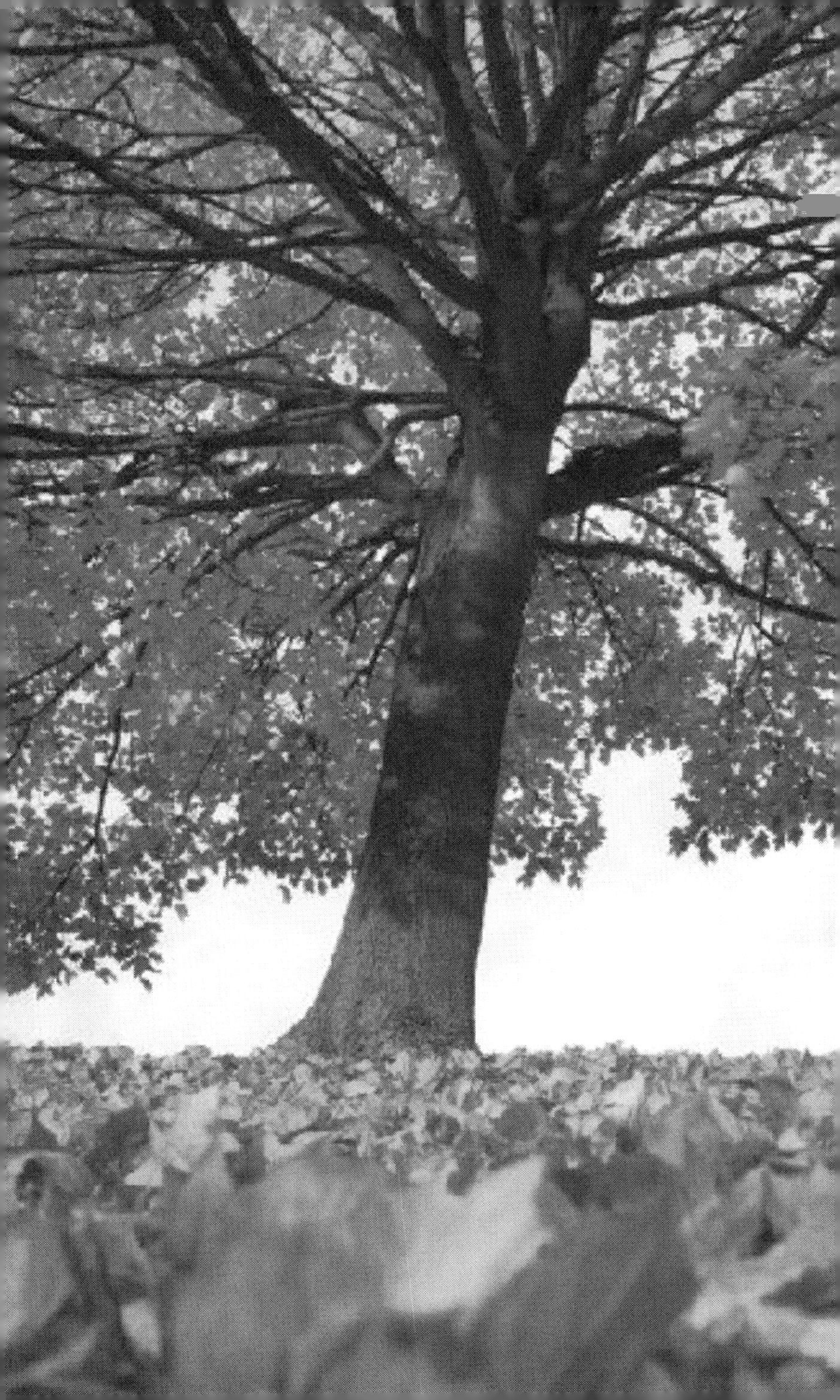

the need
to control other people
is the worst part
of human nature

it is the hardest part
to let go of

and yet the most powerful key
to true freedom

let go
of the need
for control

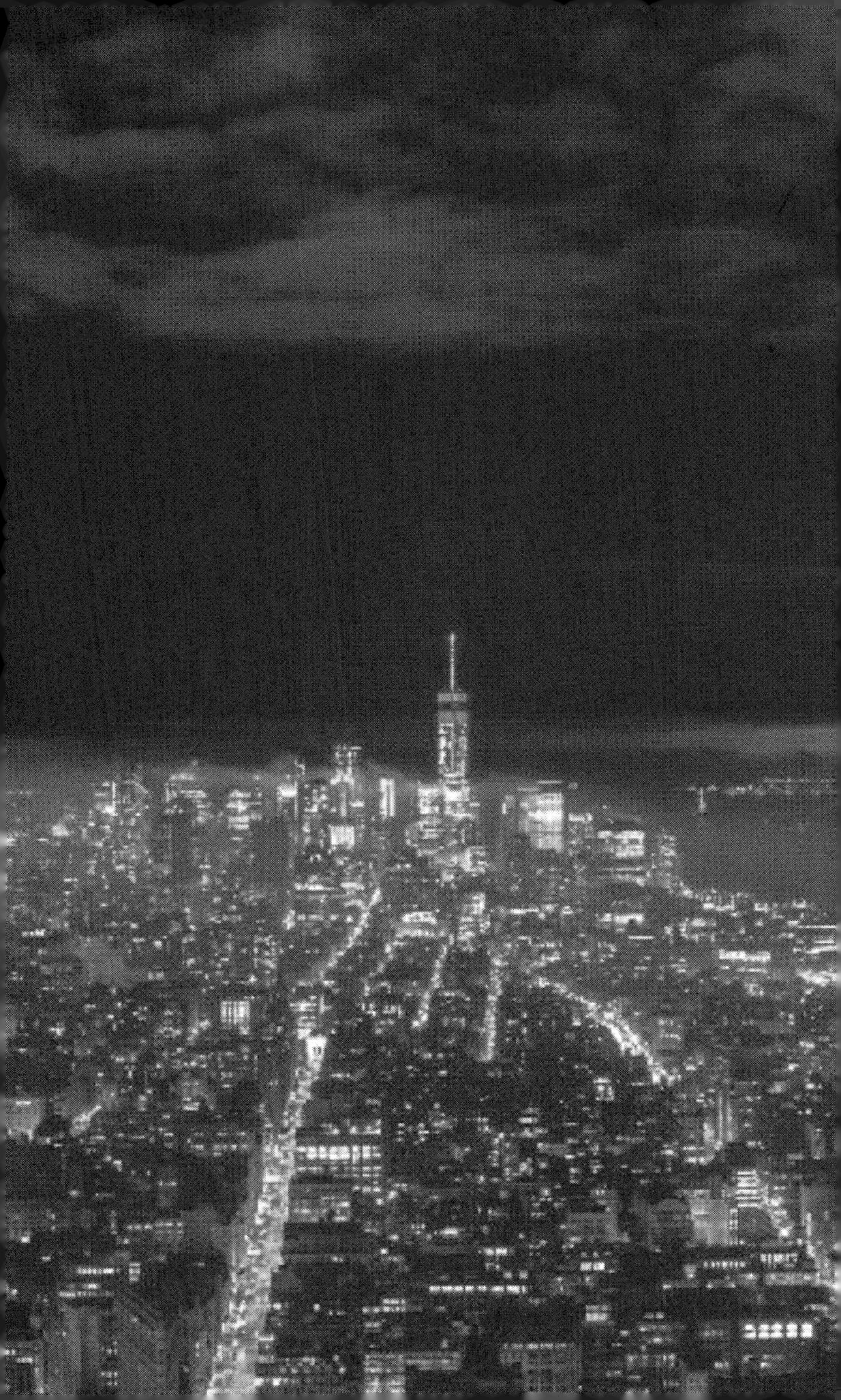

our true selves
at the deepest level
of our spirits
are unafraid of anything

it is only our bodies
which are taught survival
that teach us
not to fly

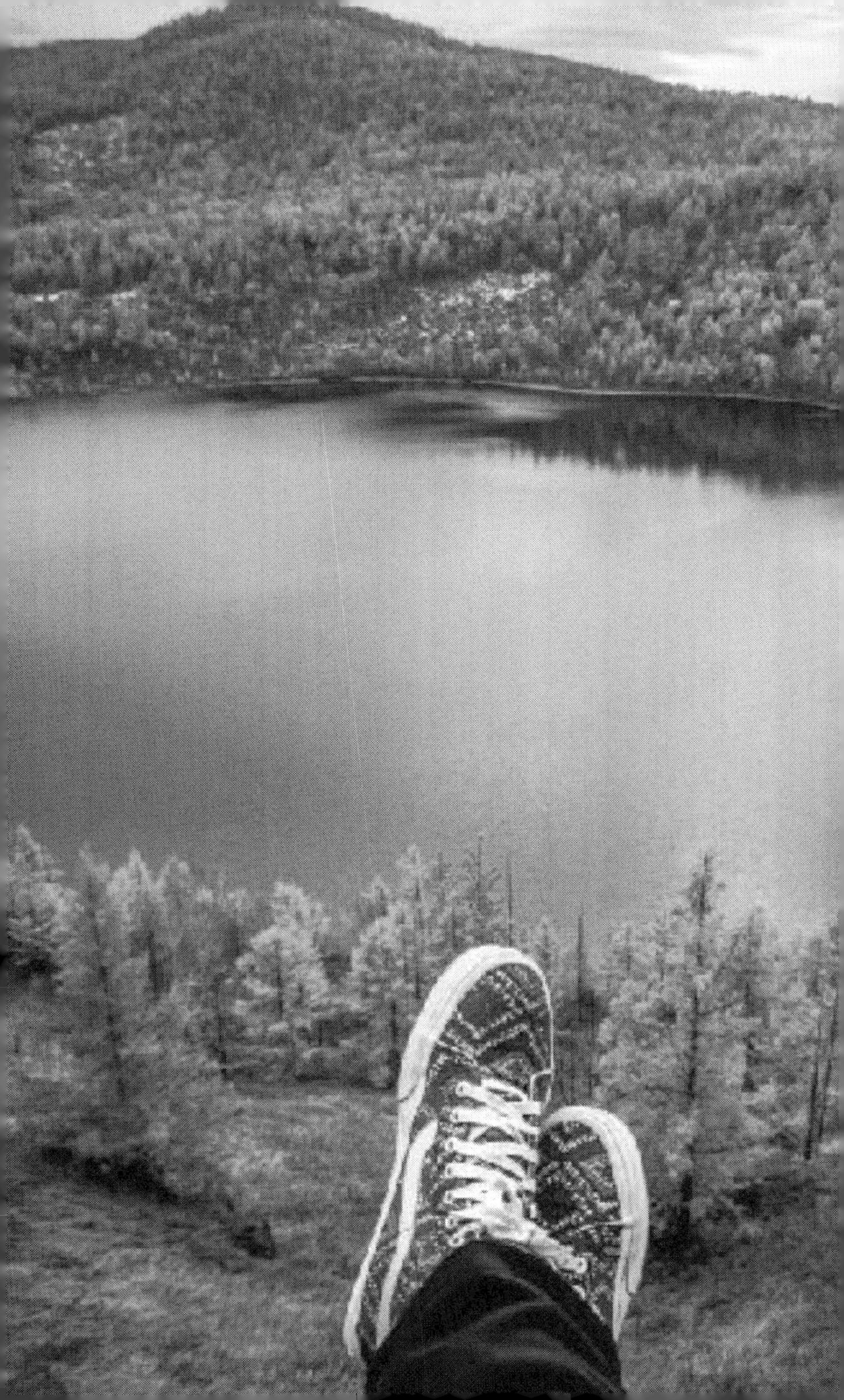

it is such a shame
that we are so often
among
crowds of people

and yet each of us
is somehow
alone.

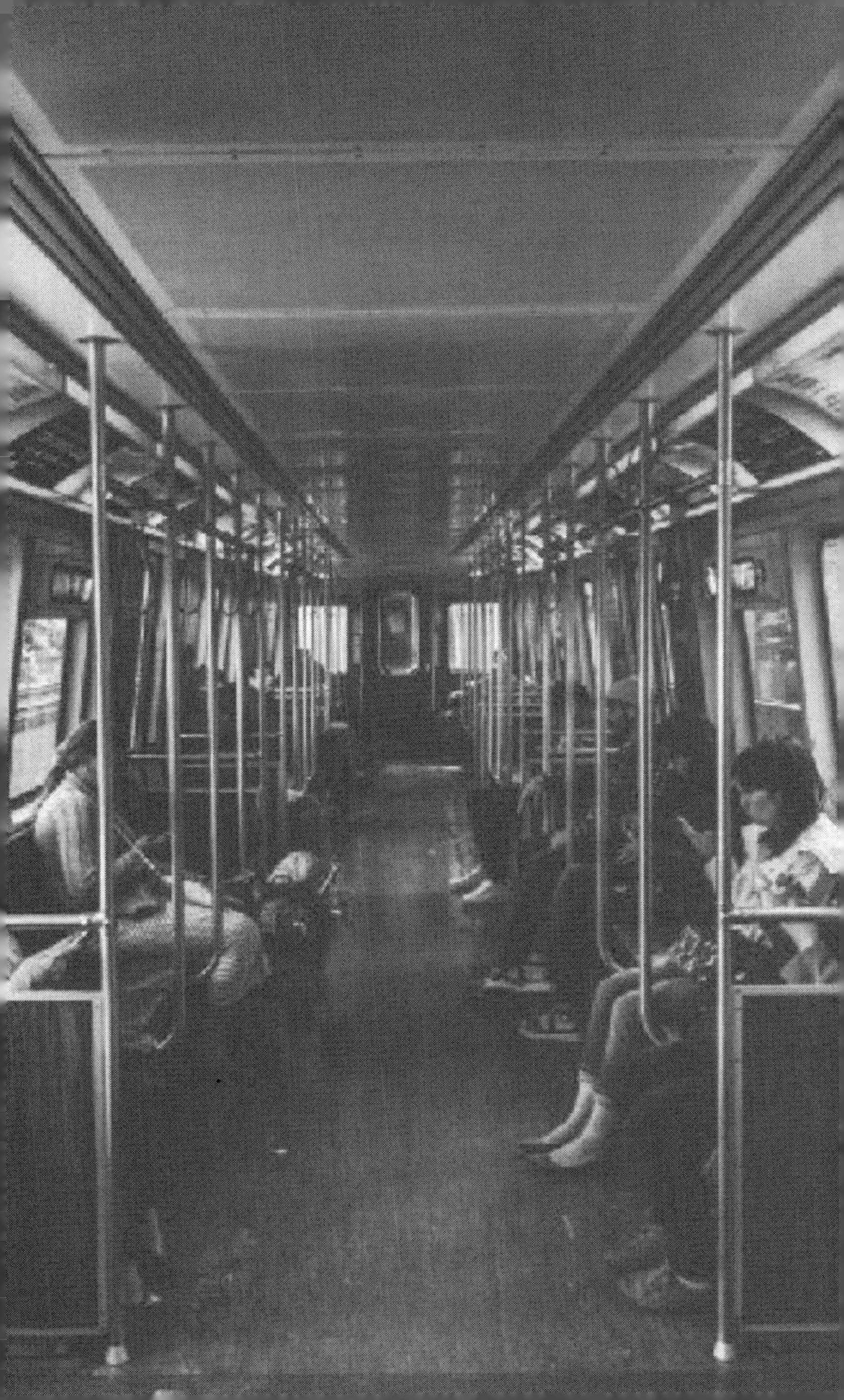

remember to encourage your friends
when they pursue their dreams

you need not tell them
when their dreams
are unrealistic

your job
is to support them
and help them
grow their wings

the world is sharp enough
already
without you
adding pain to it.

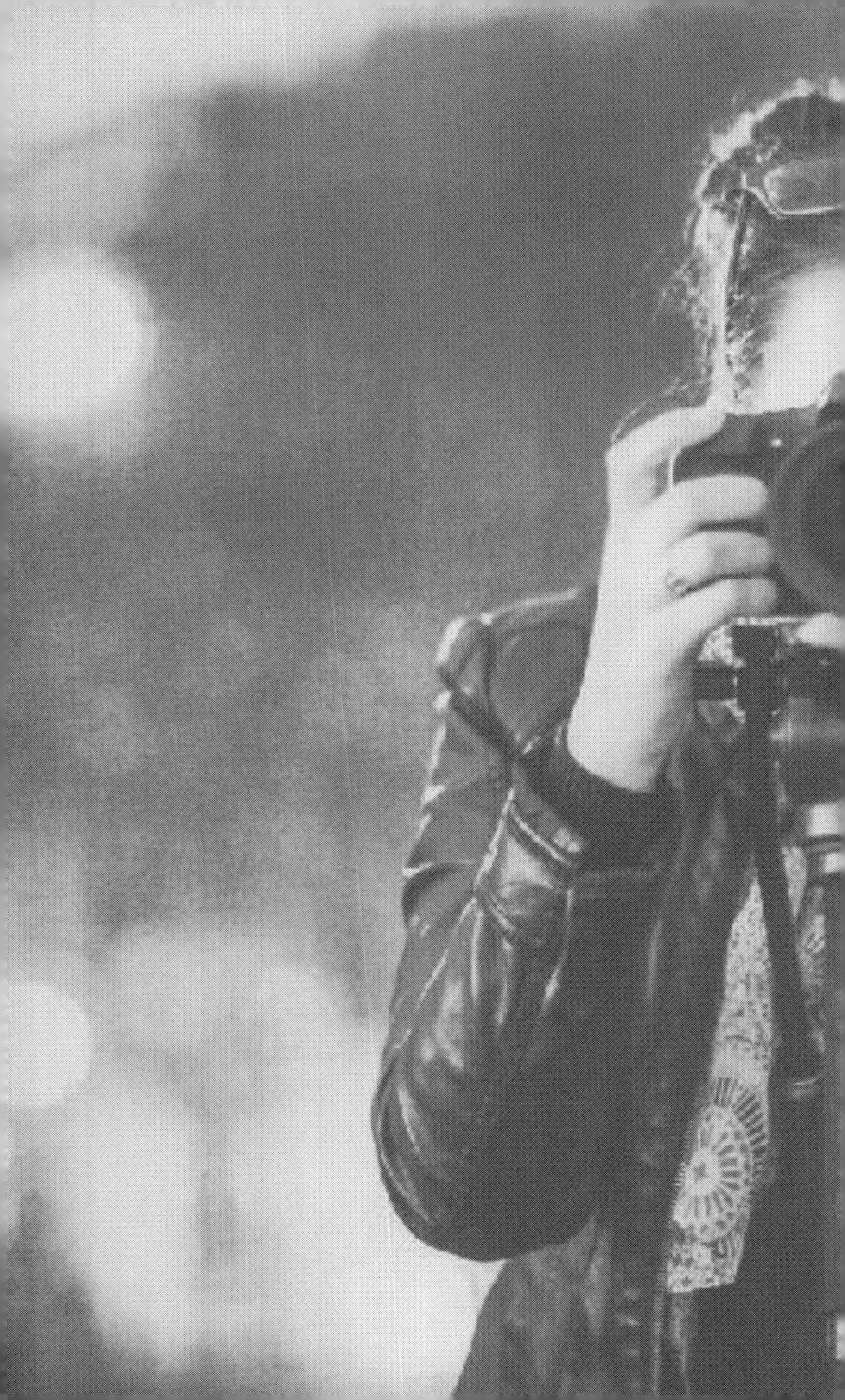

silence
is so rare
these days

and yet
so powerful.

meditate
on your life
and take some time
to find some silence
today.

a mind
which has not travelled
is so limited
in the way it can grow

live a little
and travel
find your path

find your way.

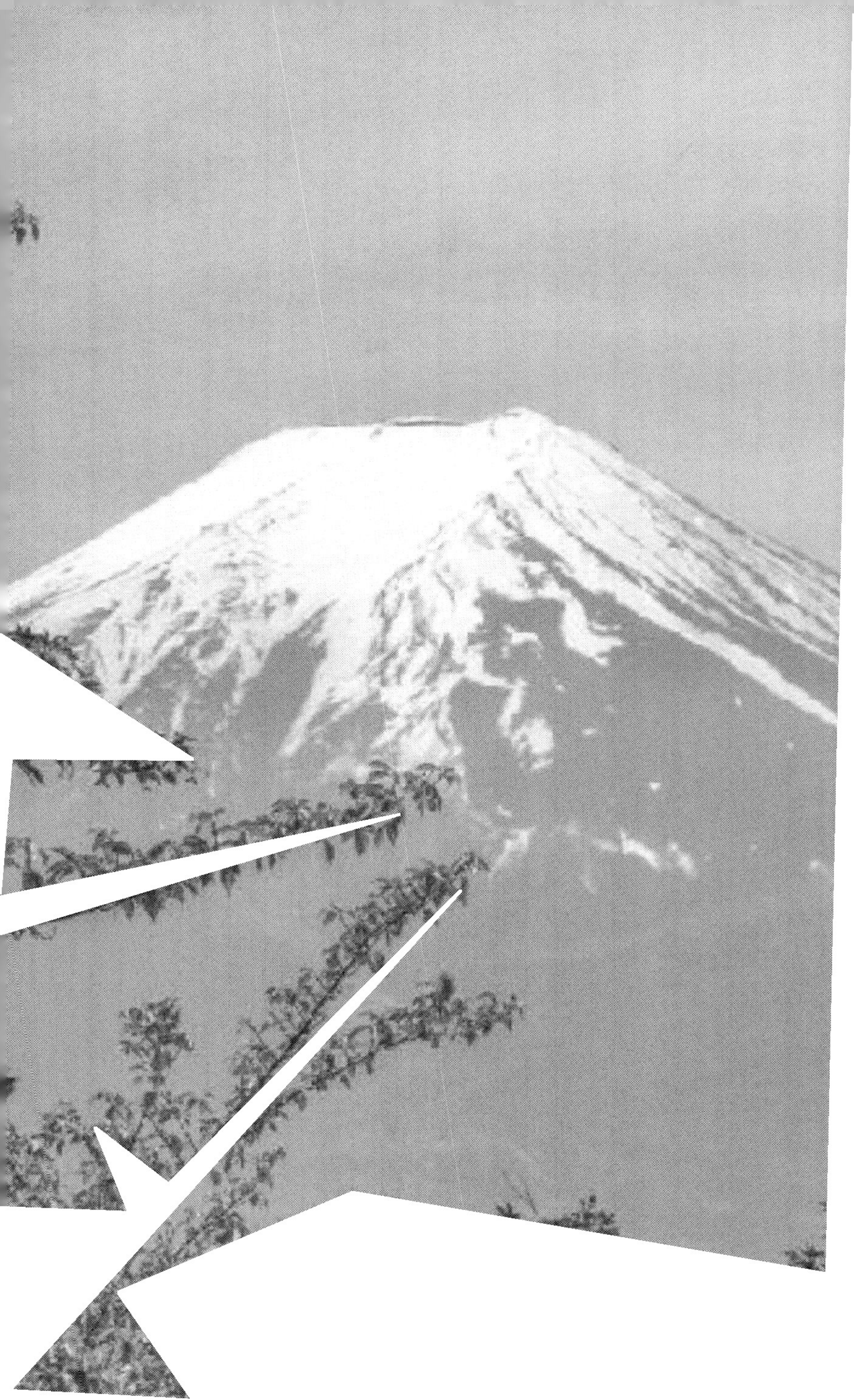

we have always been
obsessed
with our power
to overcome nature

but we would be
so much happier
if we went with nature
instead of against it.

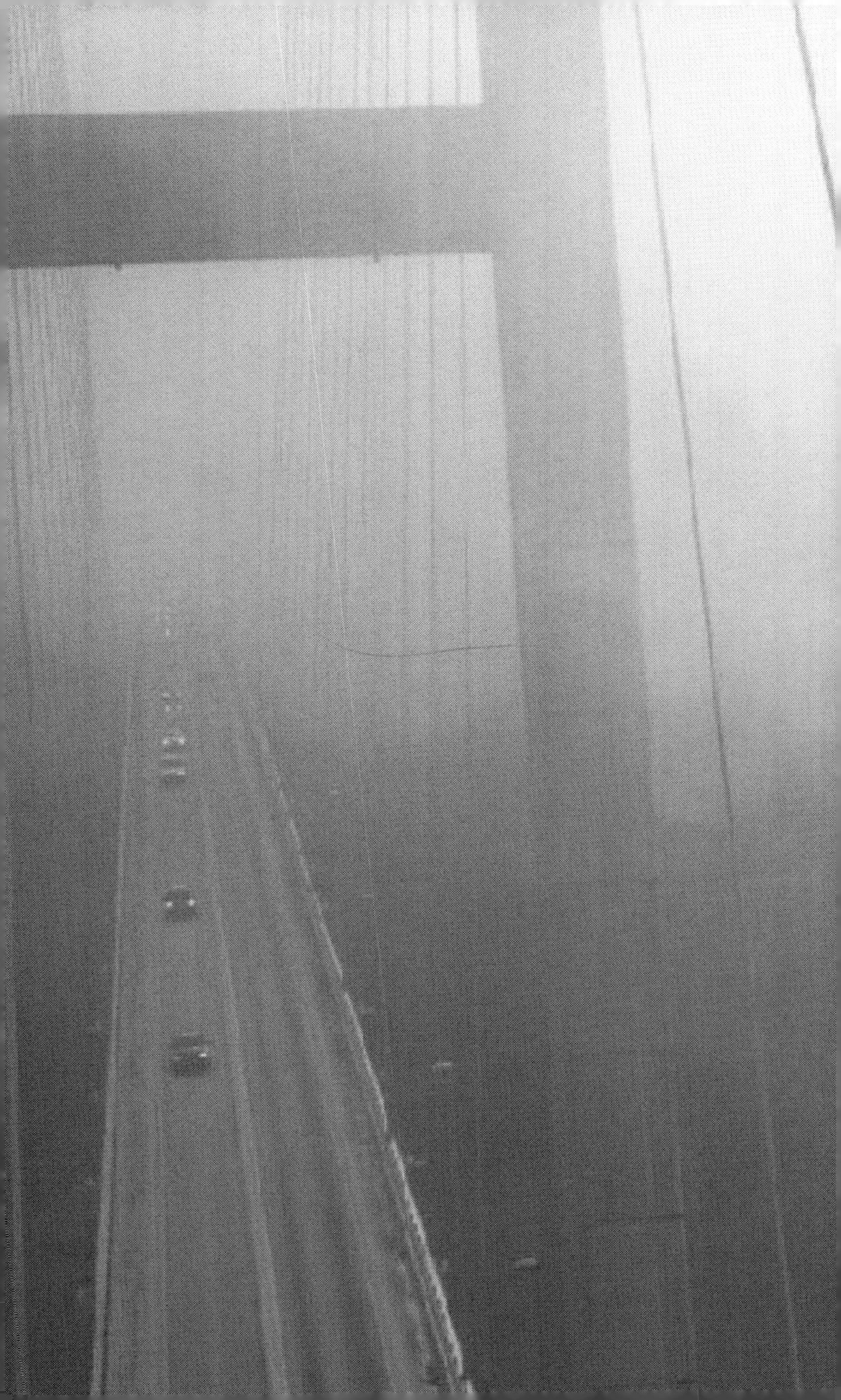

some roads
are meant to end

and that
is one of the hardest lessons
life teaches us.

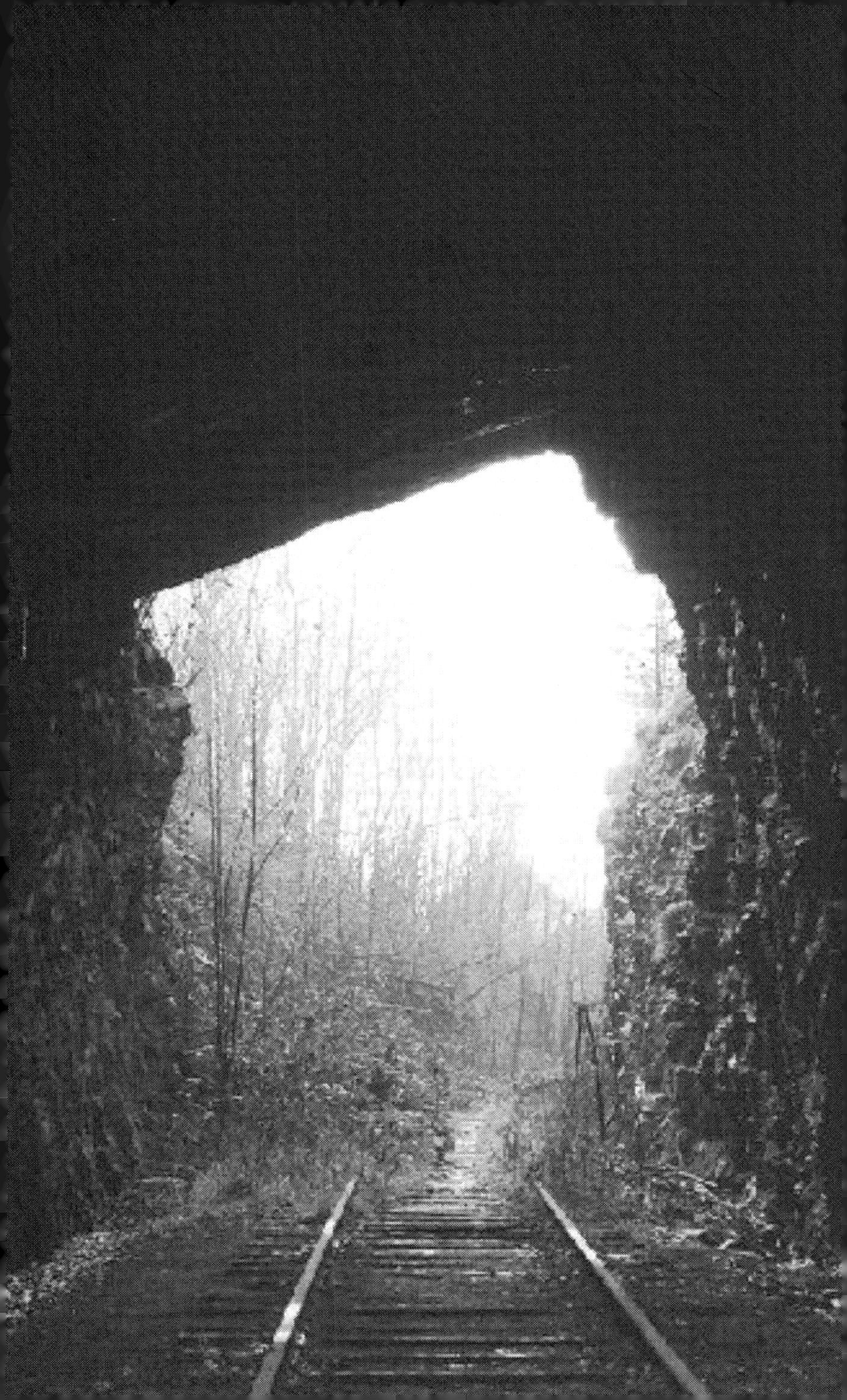

it is such a shame
that something
as beautiful
as religion
which teaches peace
and love

has been twisted
by greedy charlatans
who use it as a weapon
of hate and gain.

CHAPTER THREE

VIBRATIONS

i weep
for all
the ancient stories
whose wisdom
has fallen
by the wayside of history
dooming us
to live
without
these powerful secrets.

there's a reason that society
doesn't want its members
to use psychedelics.

they want to control you
and make you
into a worker bee
who is willing
to give all this effort
for the gain of others

our true selves
know, and have always known
that there is so much more
we are meant to do
than live a life
controlled.

that is why
they try to block
the gateways
to true knowledge.

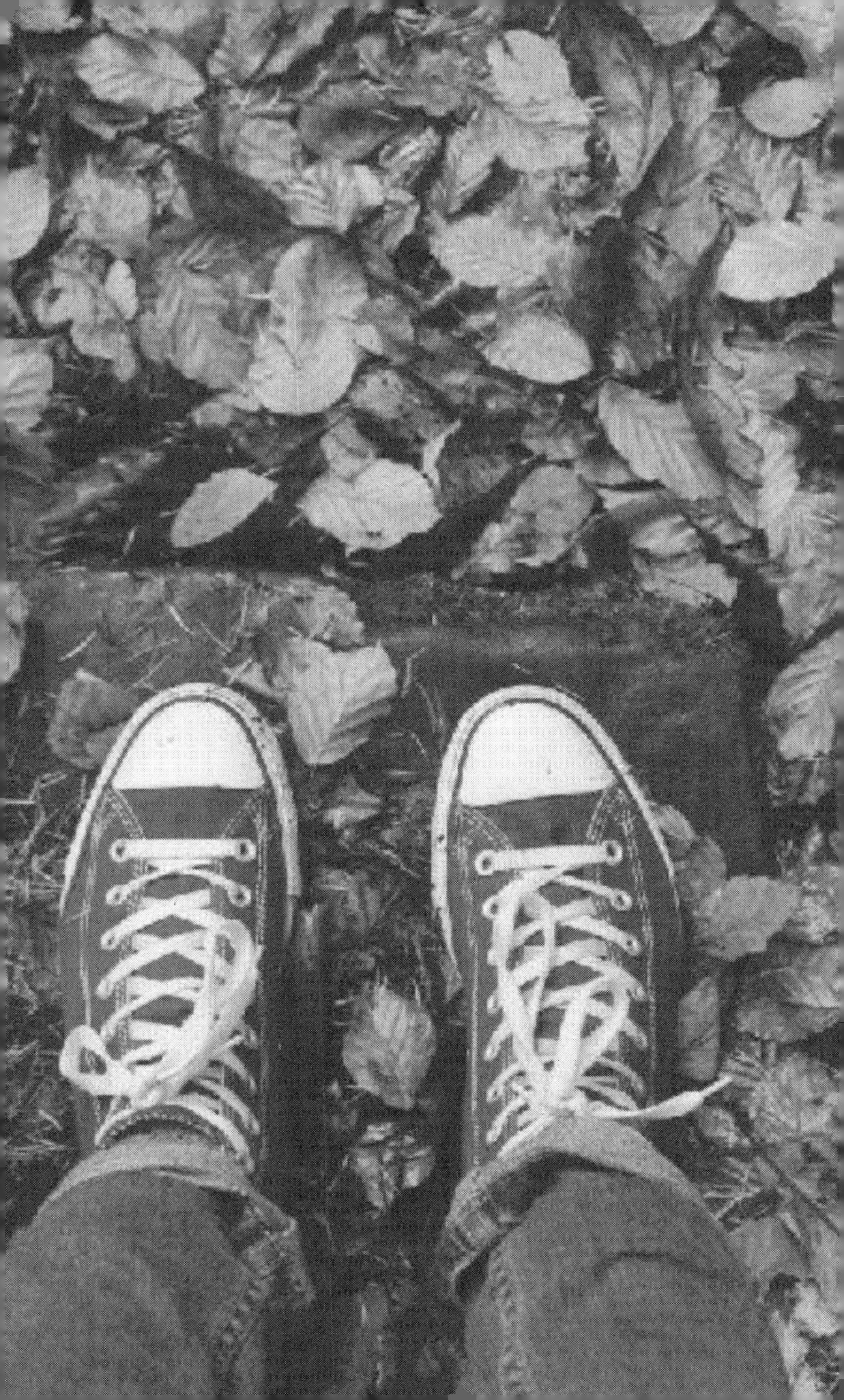

the only way
to find true healing
is to get in touch
with your deepest self.

only by drinking
from the well
of spiritual power
can you overcome
these scars.

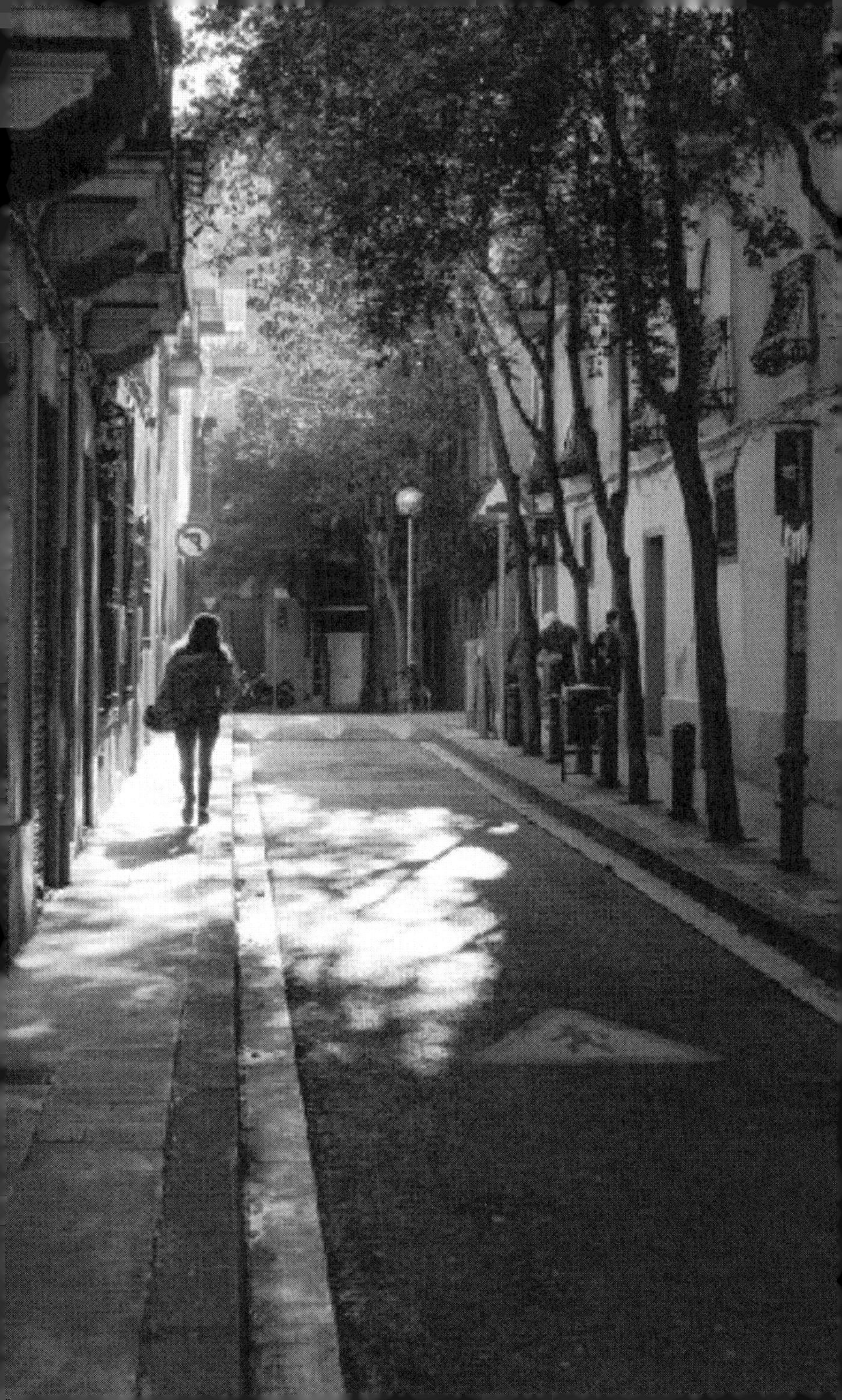

we spend so much time
looking at screens
that we have forgotten
how to look
up
at the stars

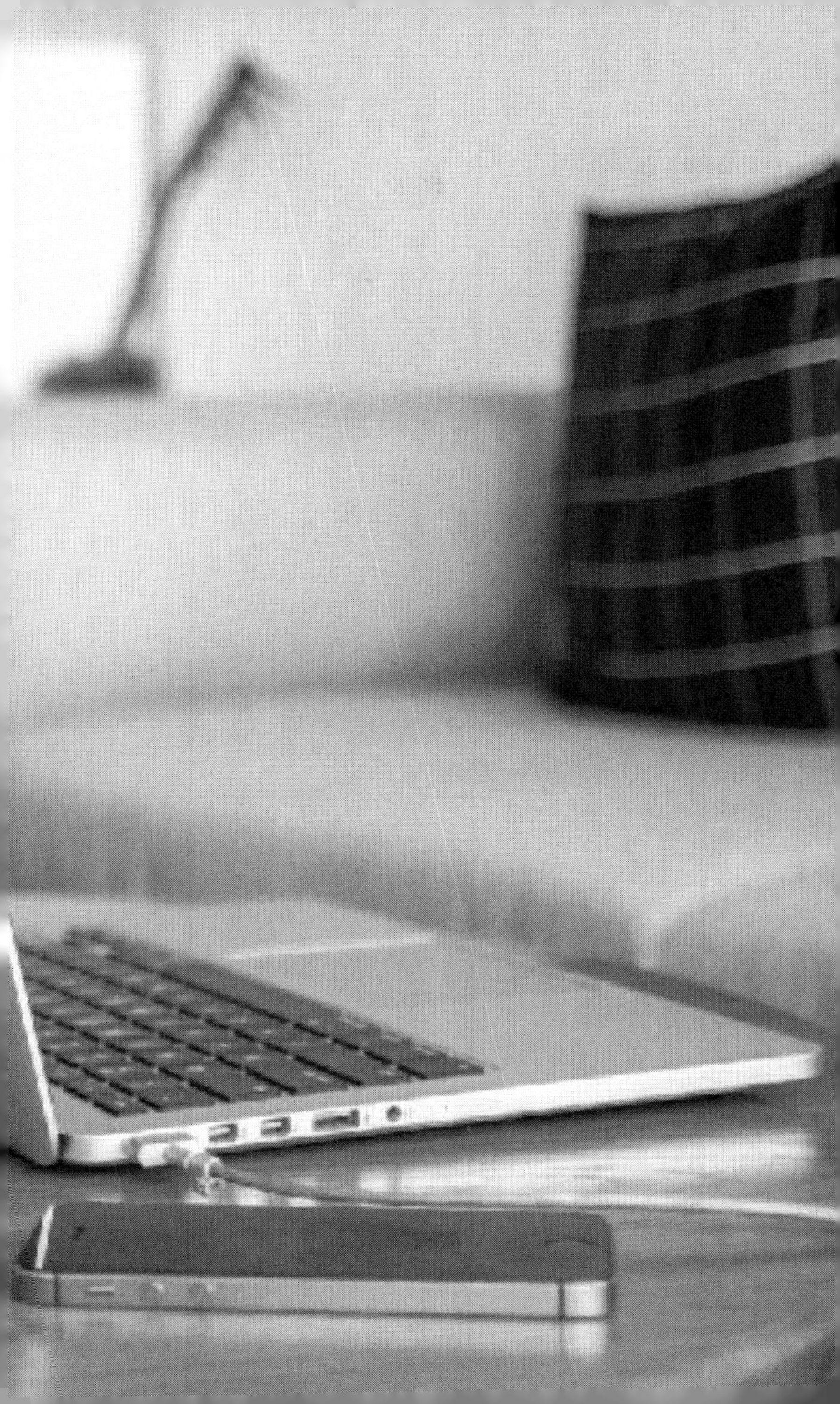

it is so important
to remember
not to judge

by judging others
we cut off
the flow of life
that we need
to be happy

one must give happiness
to give it

its the laws of spiritual physics
that apply to matter too.

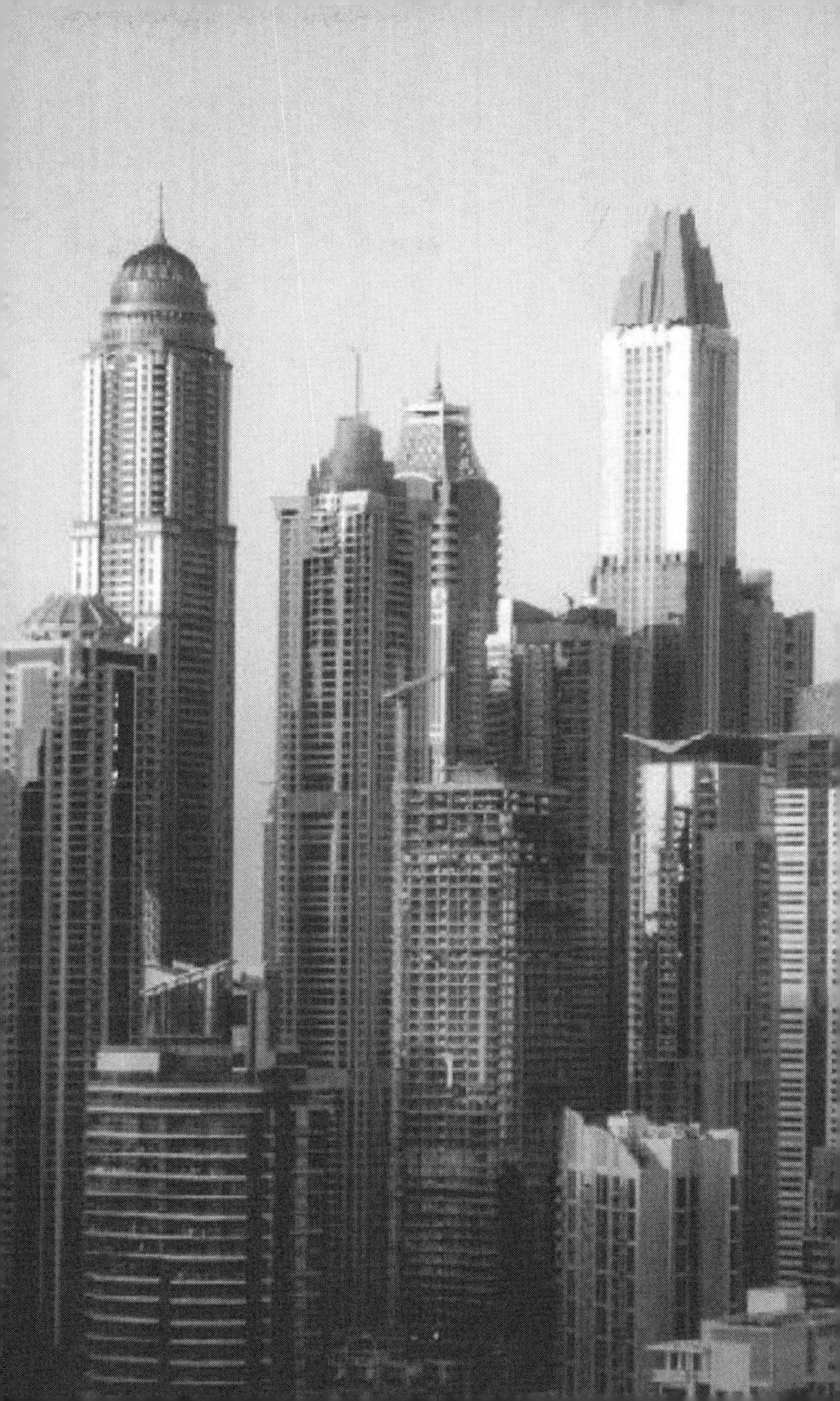

anything you want in life
can be brought to you
when you freely give it
back to the universe.

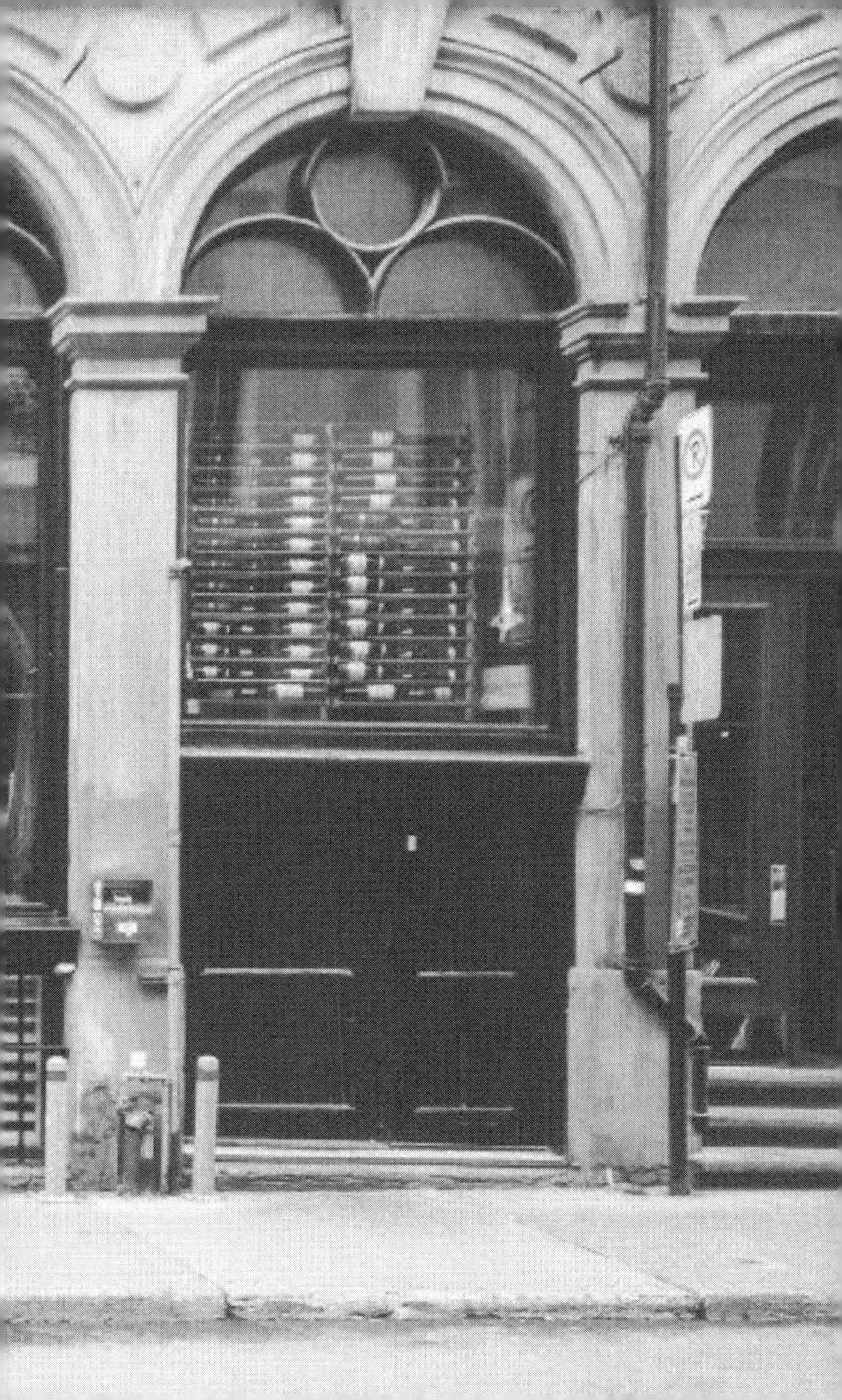

it is such a shame
that cathedrals
are a symbol of
abuse of religion
and its power

when they could
be symbols
of helping the poor
and healing humanity.

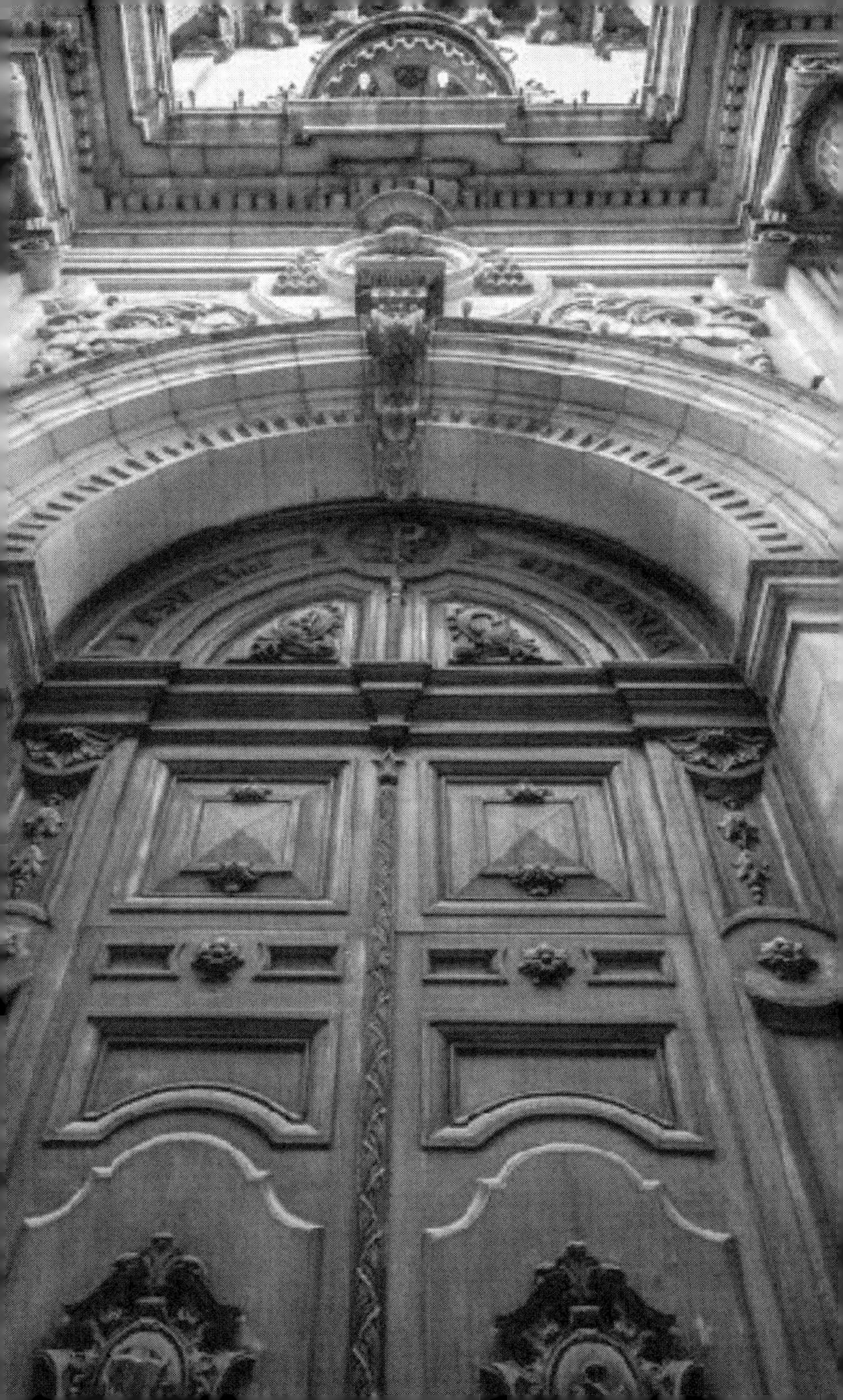

meditate
by candlelight
in a dark room

commune with the flames
and see in them
the things about yourself
that you must change
to become truly happy.

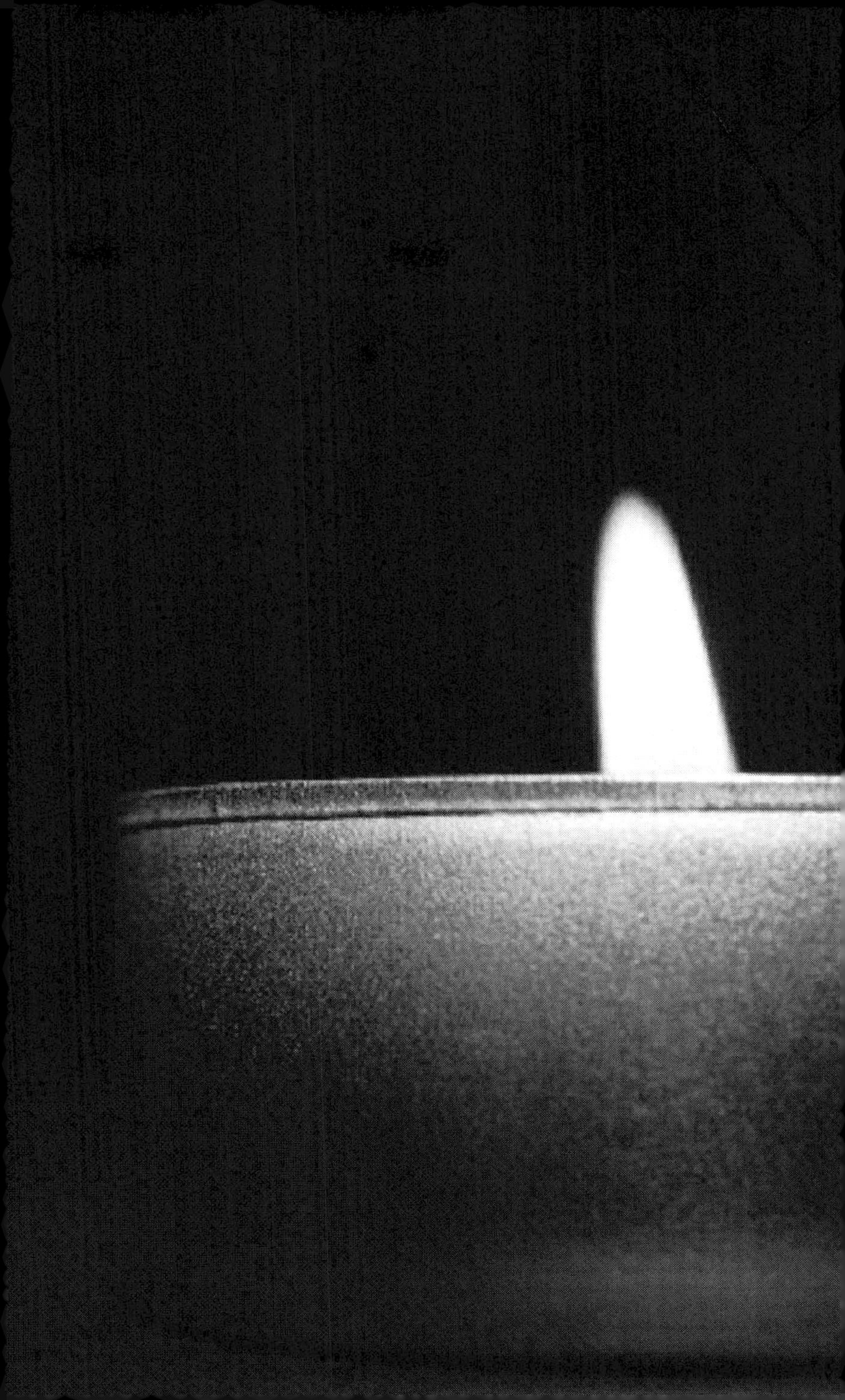

we spend so much time
defining our image
and trying to live up
to the reputation
we wish we have
that we are slowly becoming
the artifice
that we present
to the world

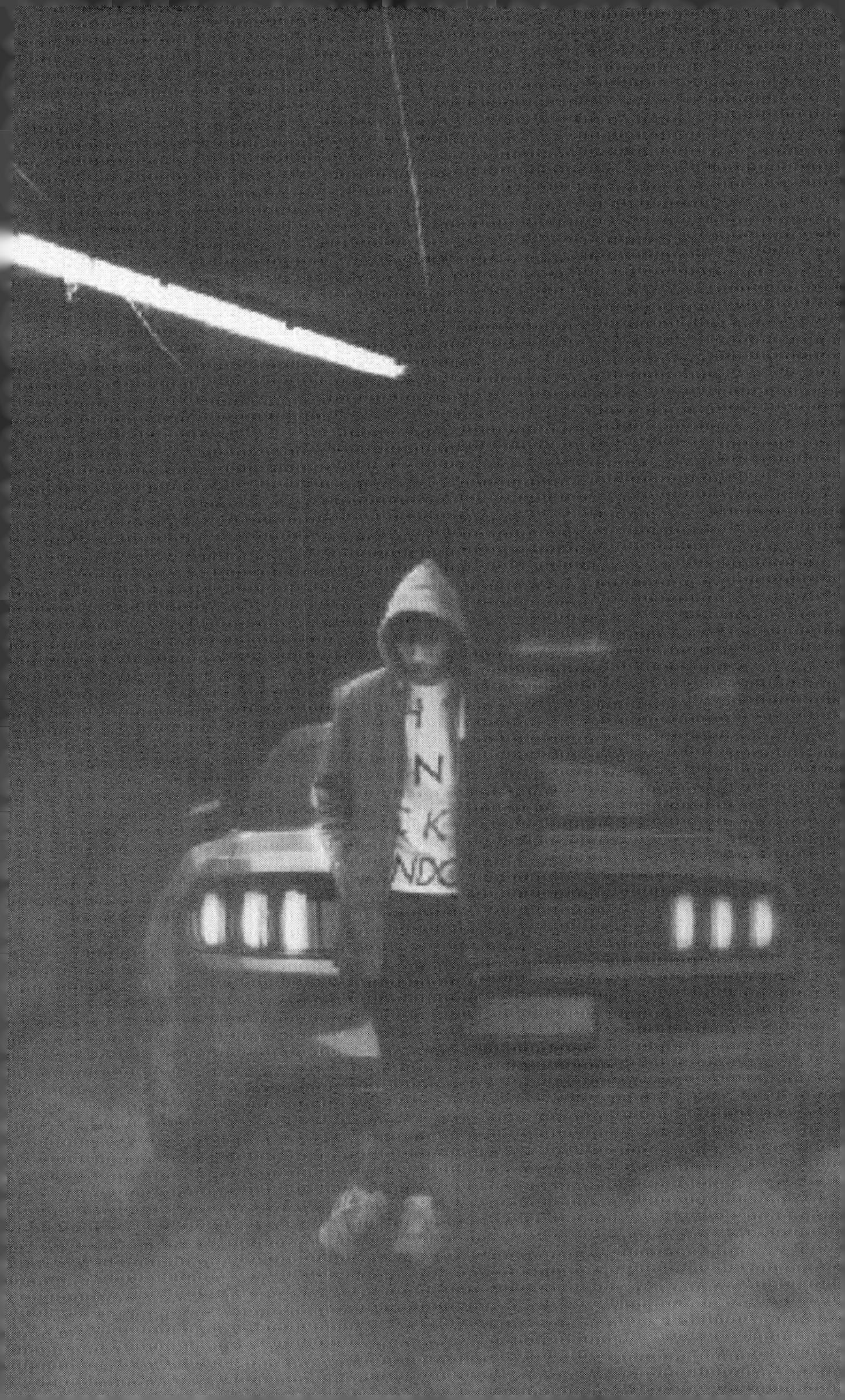

don't forget
to do something
physical
today.

it's so easy
to get caught up in screens
that we neglect
our physical bodies.

go on a walk
or a run
or anything
as long as it gets you
on your feet

it's more important
than you might think

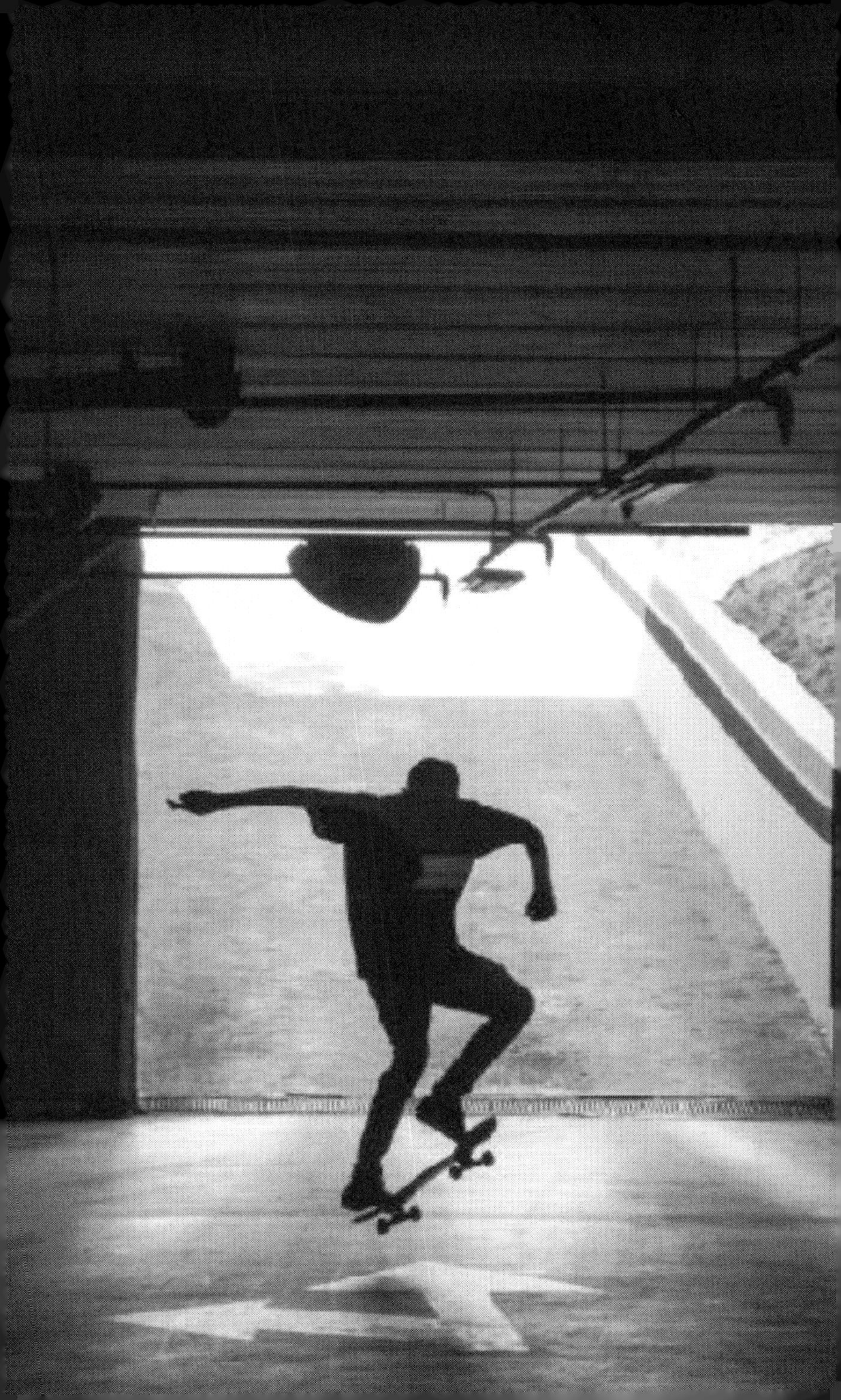

how is it
that we can build
vast cities
of concrete, glass, and steel

and yet we
somehow cannot
guarantee healthcare
for our own flesh
and blood?

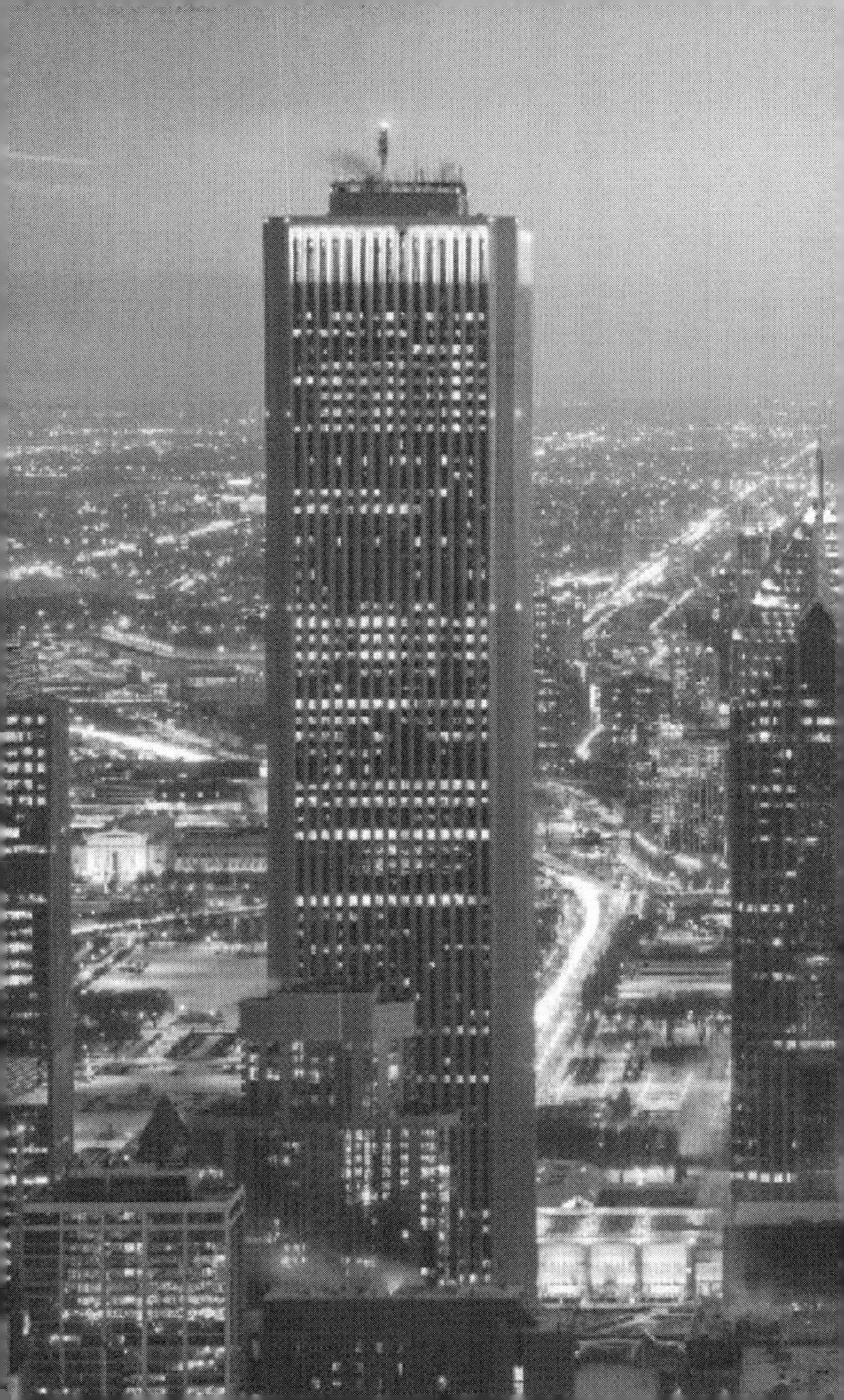

our paths
are not set in stone
and destiny
is a fluid thing

there is still time
to undo your mistakes
and live a life
of true freedom

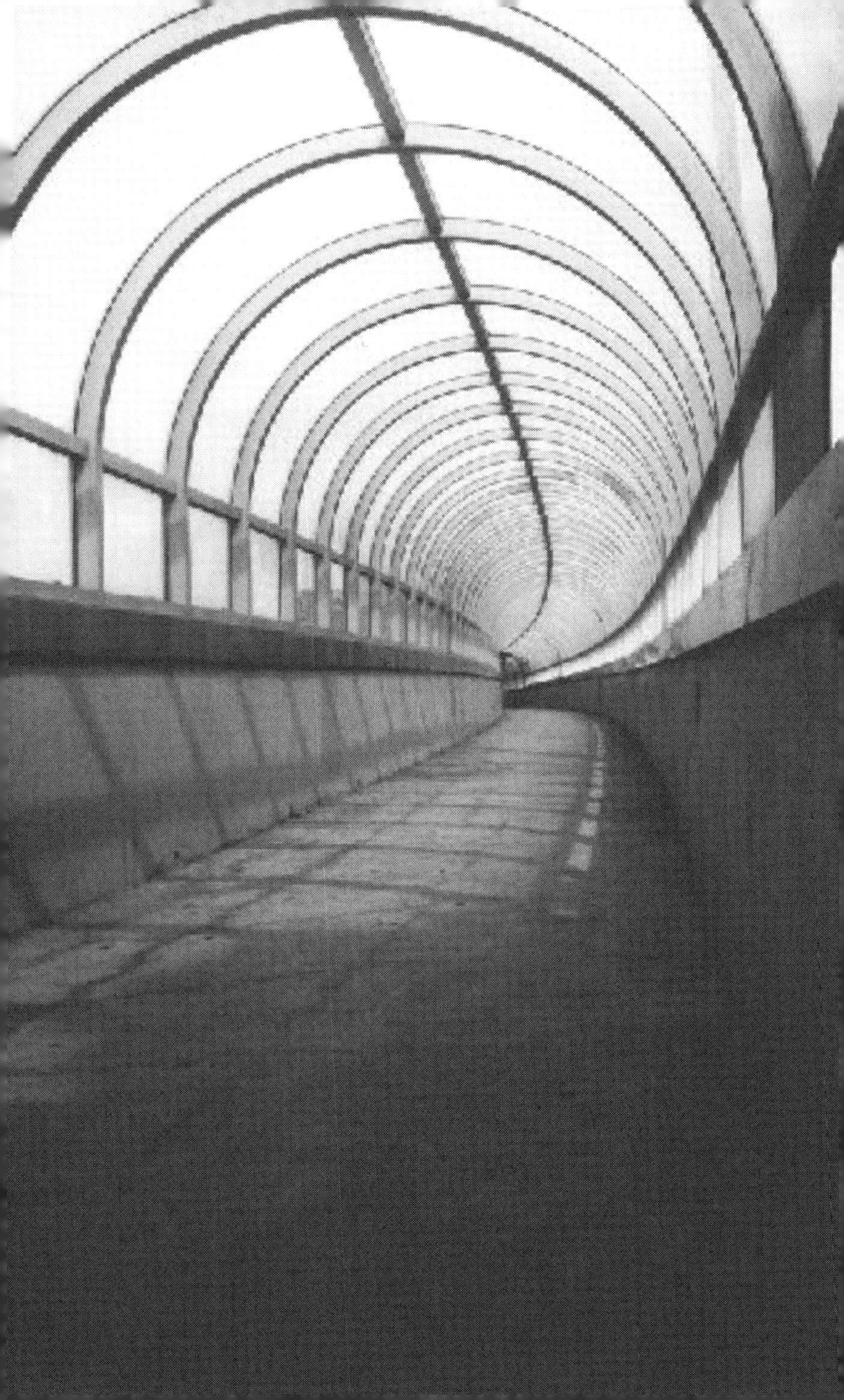

there is something
so important
about socializing
in person
with another human being

we draw strength and power
from those around us
and it's important
to not be
so caught up
in social media
that we forget
to be social.

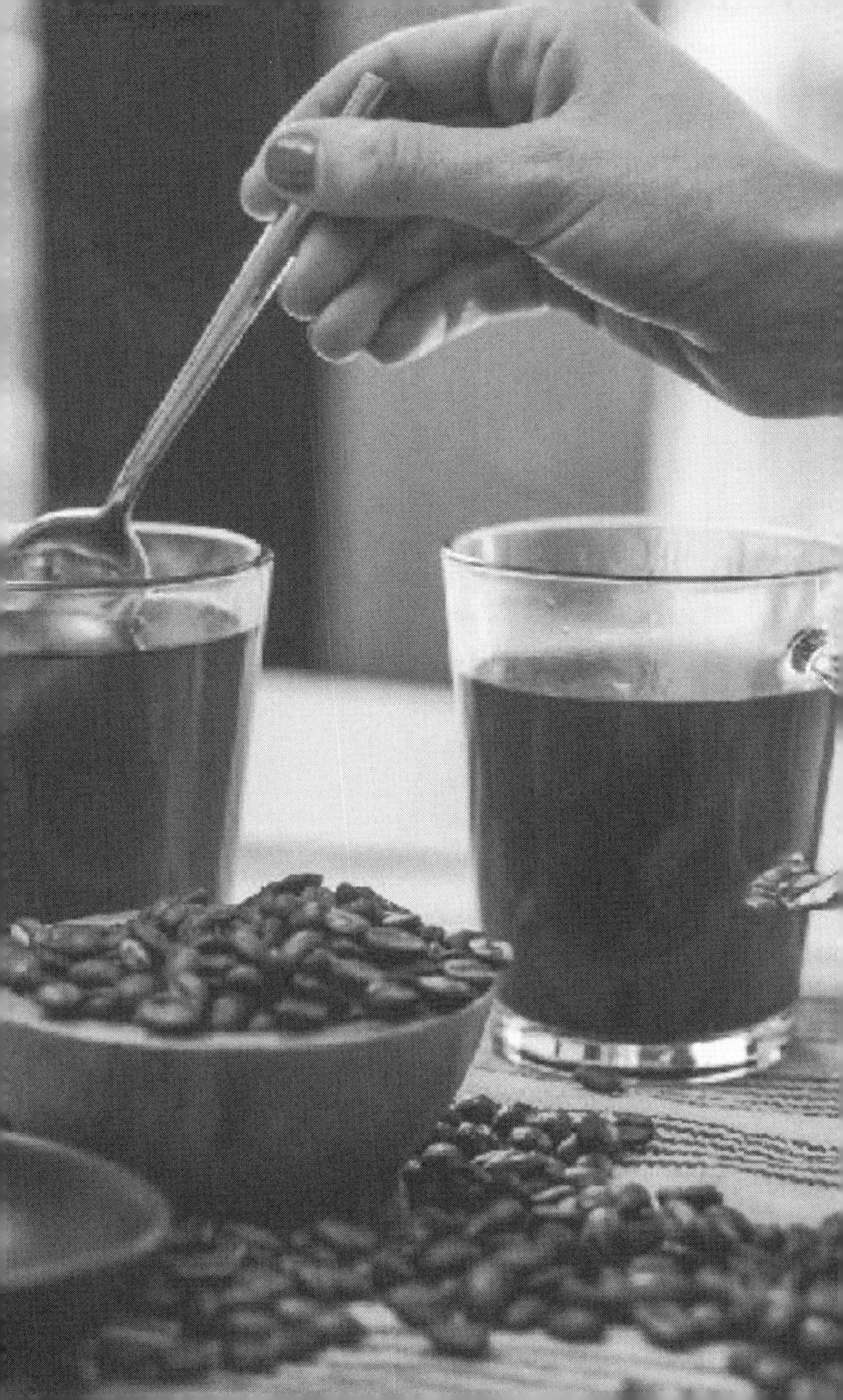

choices
are not as complicated
as we often think.

always choose
the path
that leads
to the most happiness
for you
and those around you

listen to your inner self
for it already knows
the right way
to go.

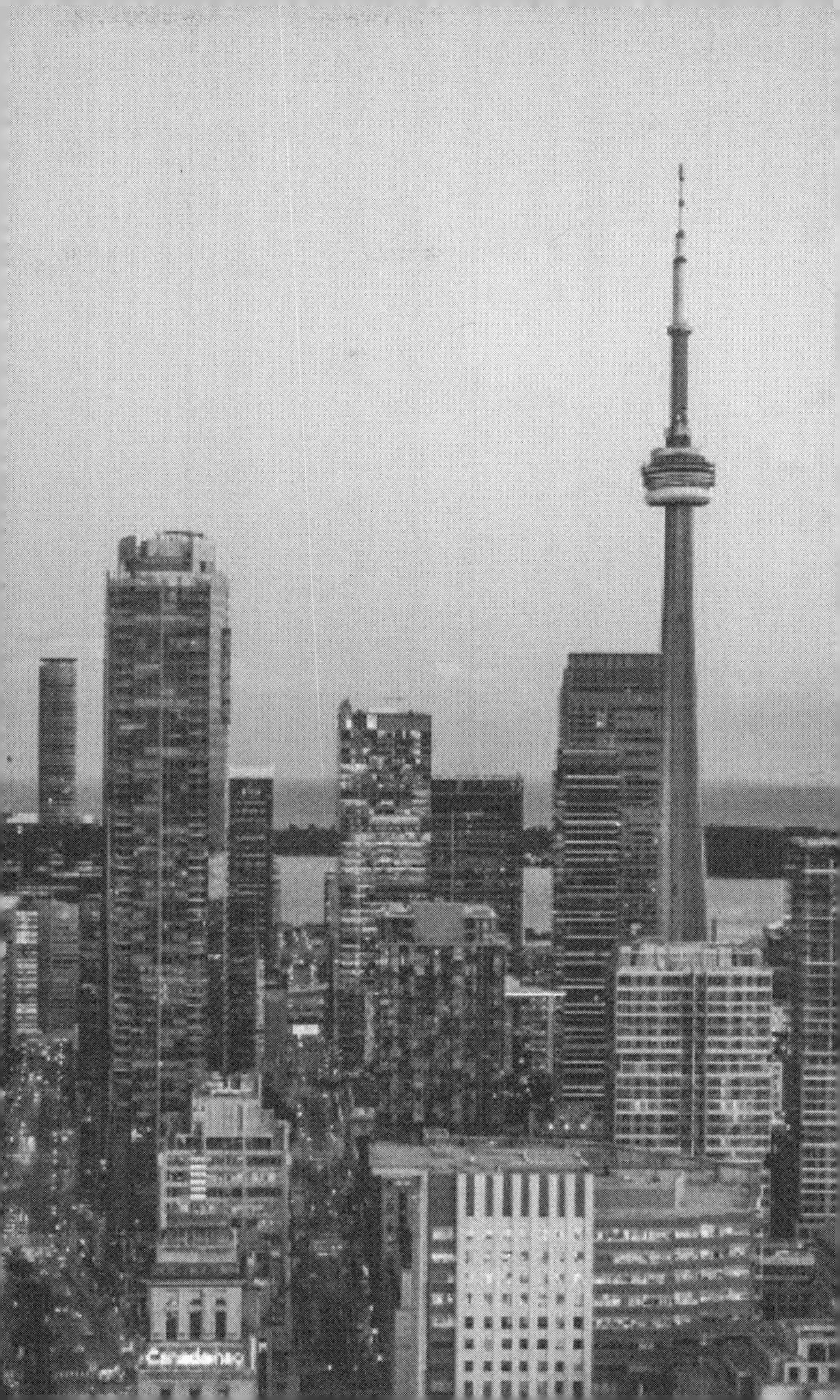

CHAPTER FOUR

CONNECTED

walk with me
through the city

let's talk
about everything
together
from sunrise
until sunset

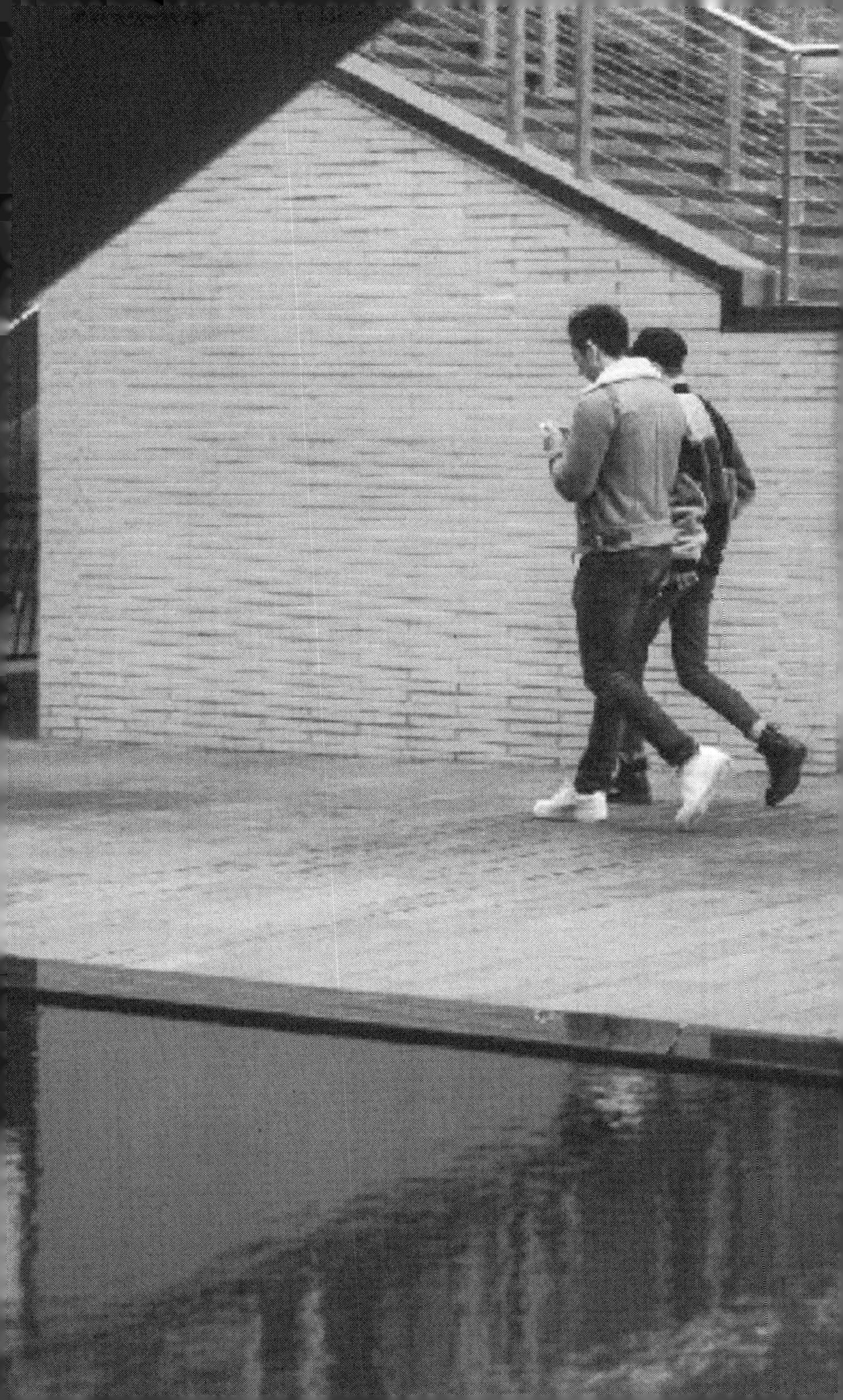

you are the light
in my life
that keeps me sane
and makes me feel
like this world
isn't quite as dark
as i used to think

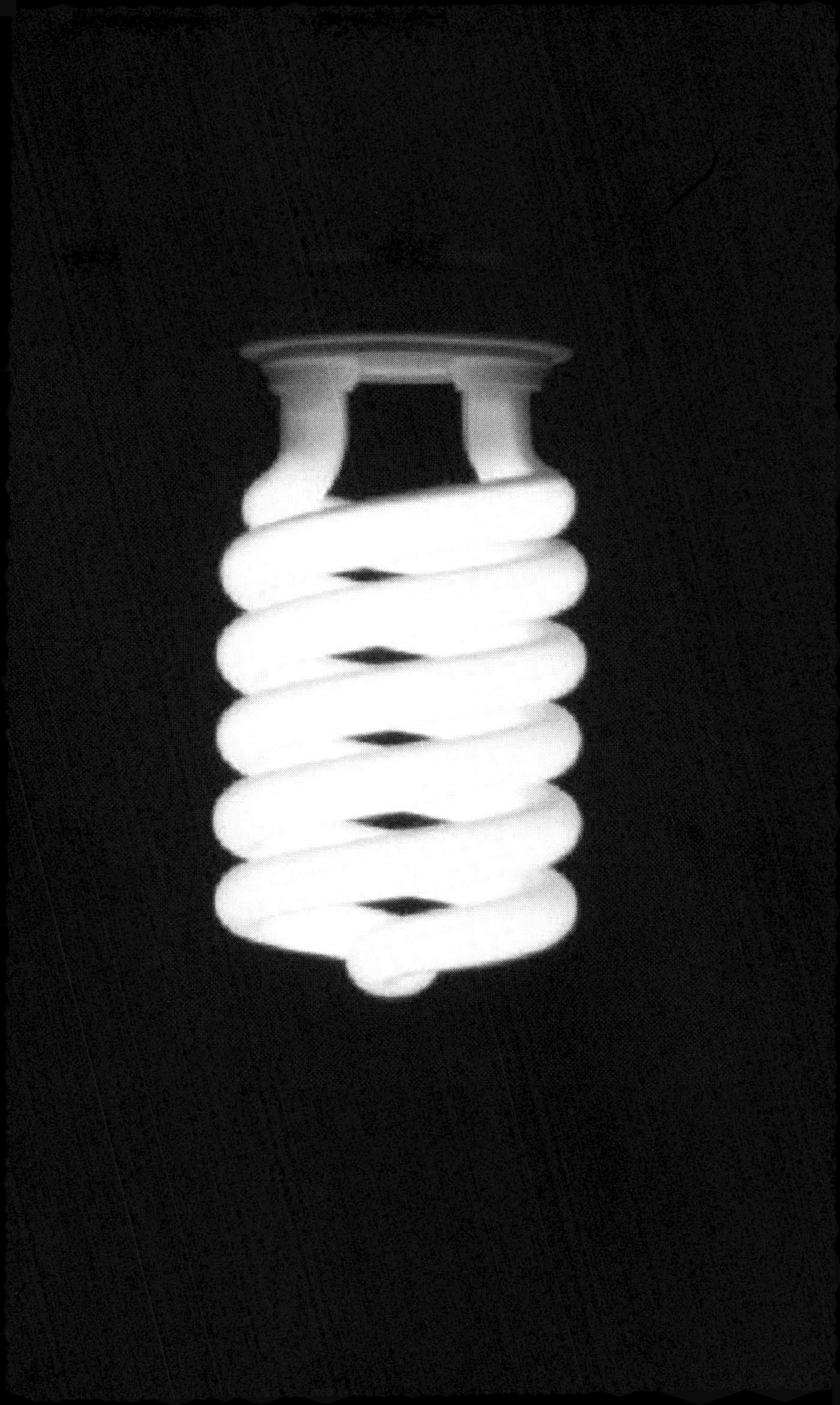

it is important
to pay
your karmic debts.

go to those
who you have hurt
in the past
and ask
for their forgiveness
—and forgive them too.

we can never be happy
while we still have
karmic debts

and there is so much happiness
to be gained
from forgiving and forgetting.

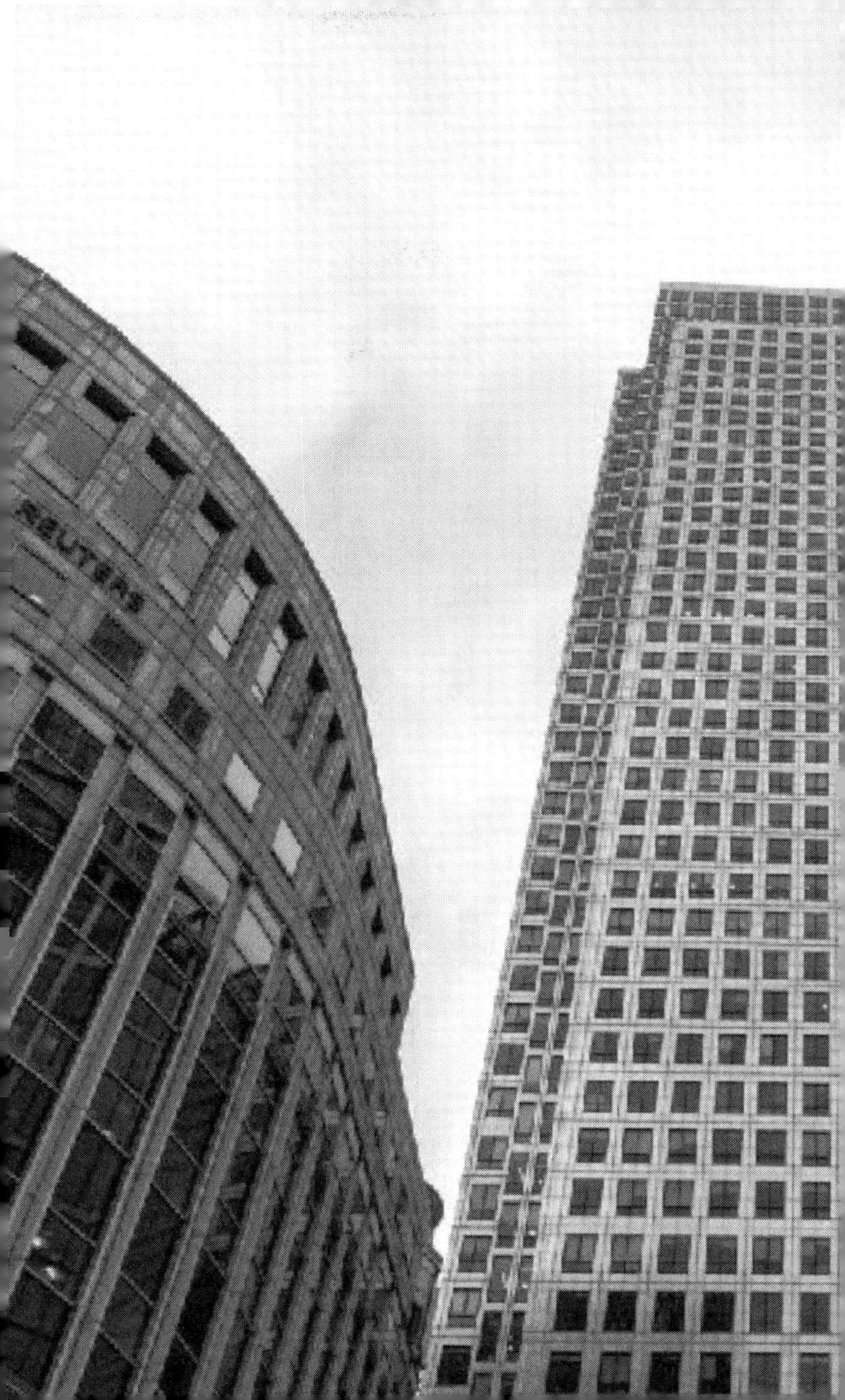
REUTERS

we are one
with the sun
and the moon
and the stars

we are one
with gravity
and time

we are one
with the universe

and we are so much
more powerful
than we think.

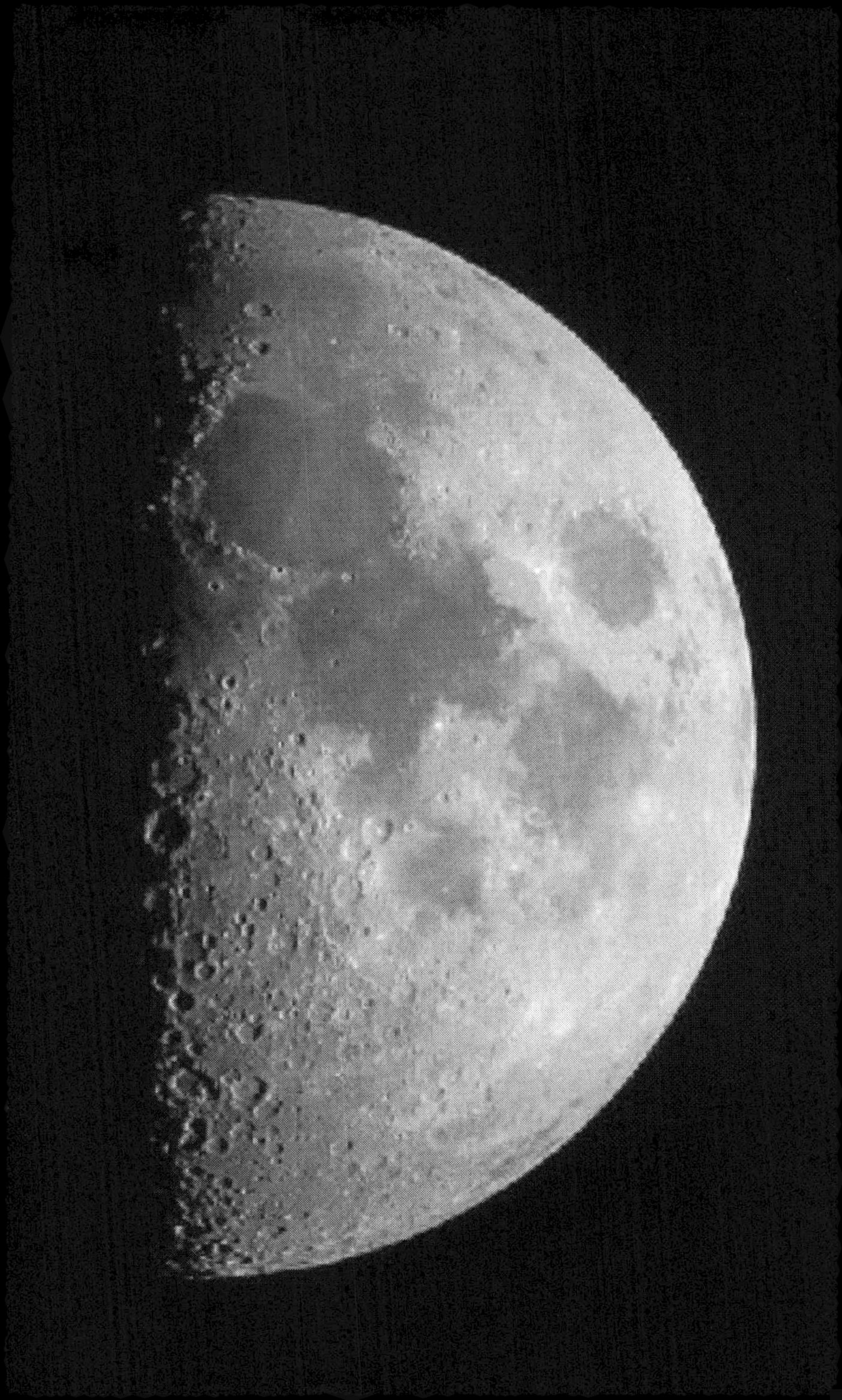

we chained our lock
onto that bridge
vowing to love each other
forever and ever

ask your heart
for guidance
in every choice
you make.

if you feel
uncomfortable
with one choice
that's how your heart
tells you
that's the wrong one.

your heart already knows
what the mind
can only guess at.

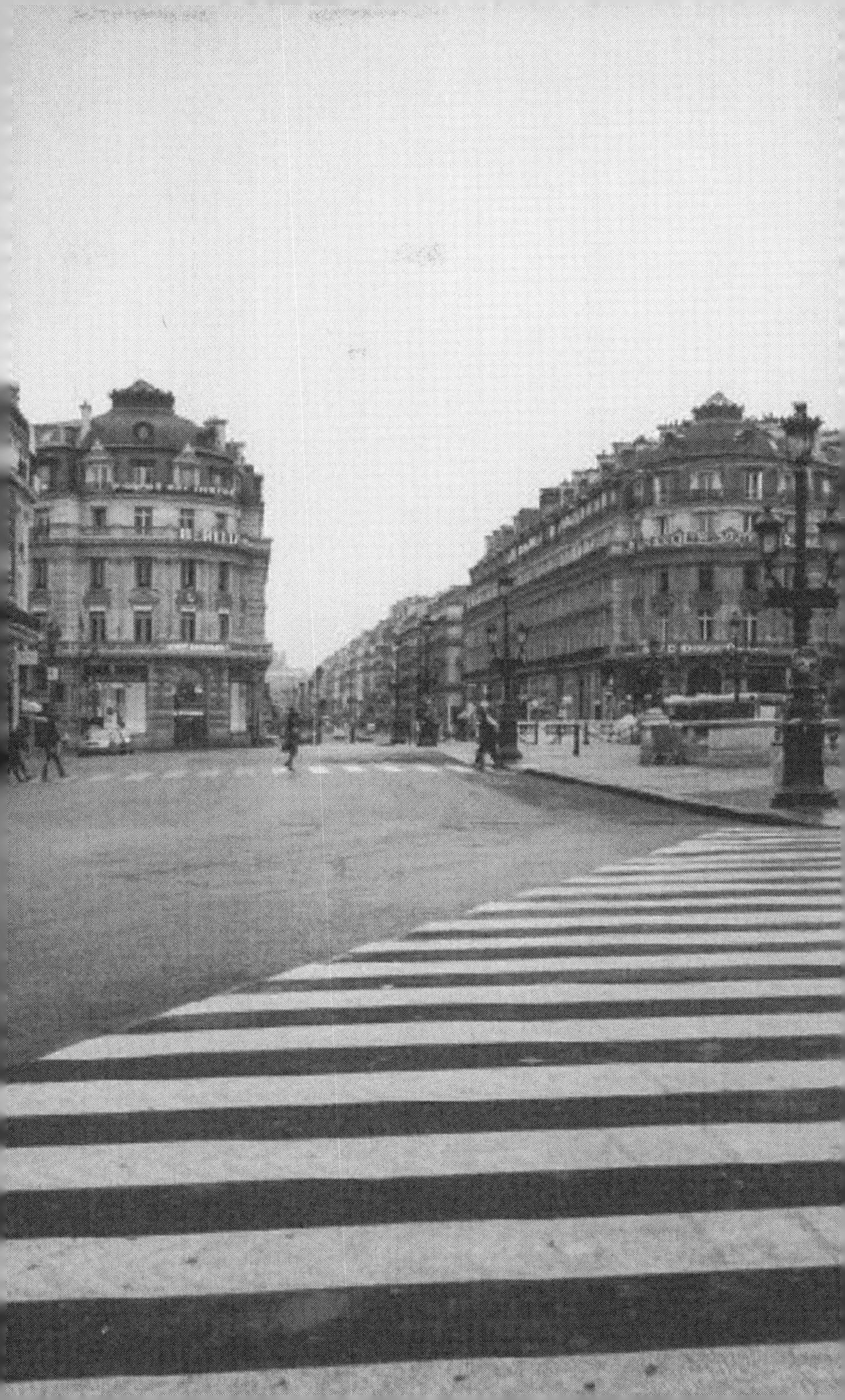

reach for the stars
and pull them down

enter into the mystery
of our cosmic existence

fall in love
with the harmony of everything

and find bliss
in finding your true nature.

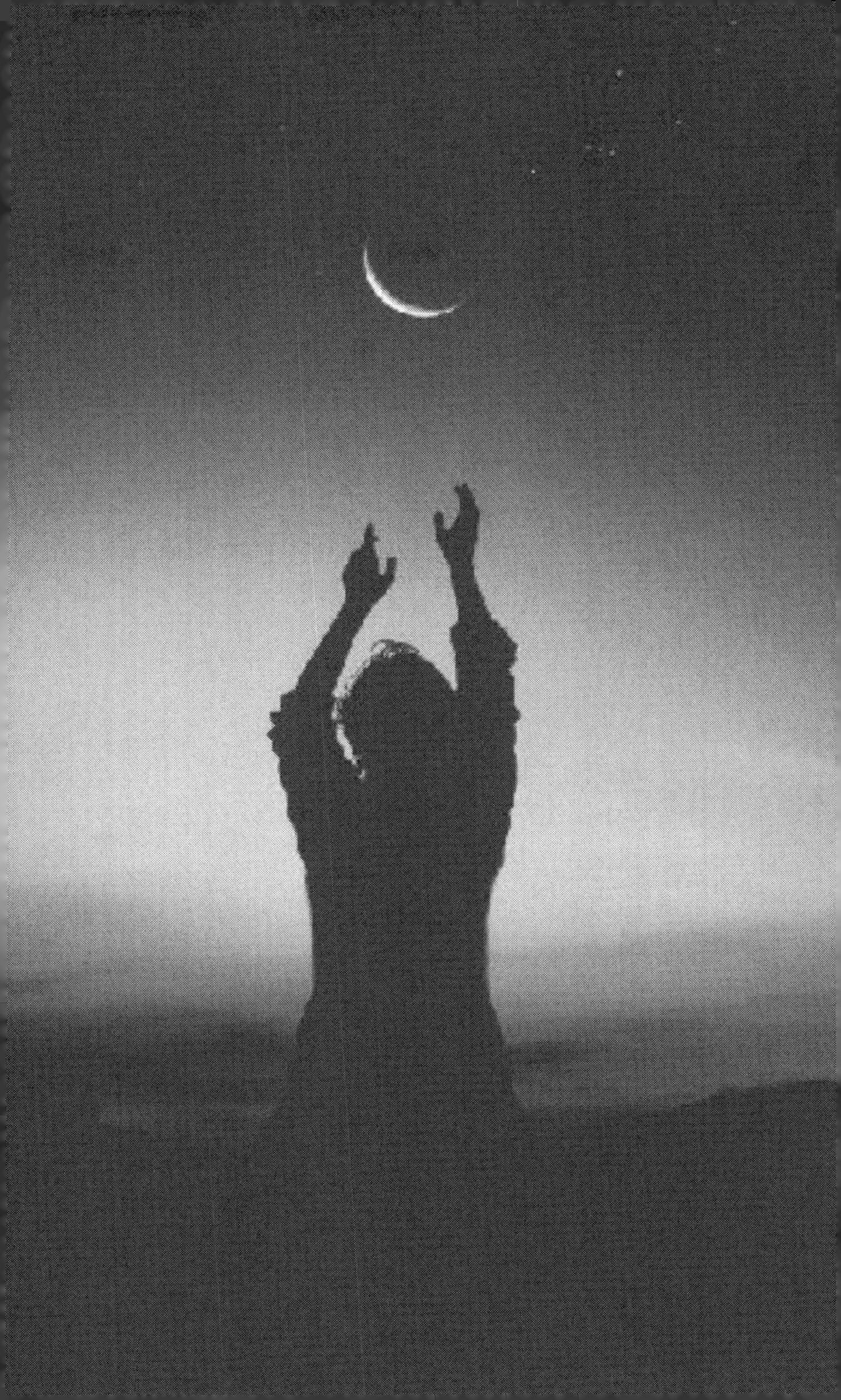

the seeds of miracles
are planted
when we give love
freely
to those around us

the universe
will give you
what you need
when you give the same
to those around you.

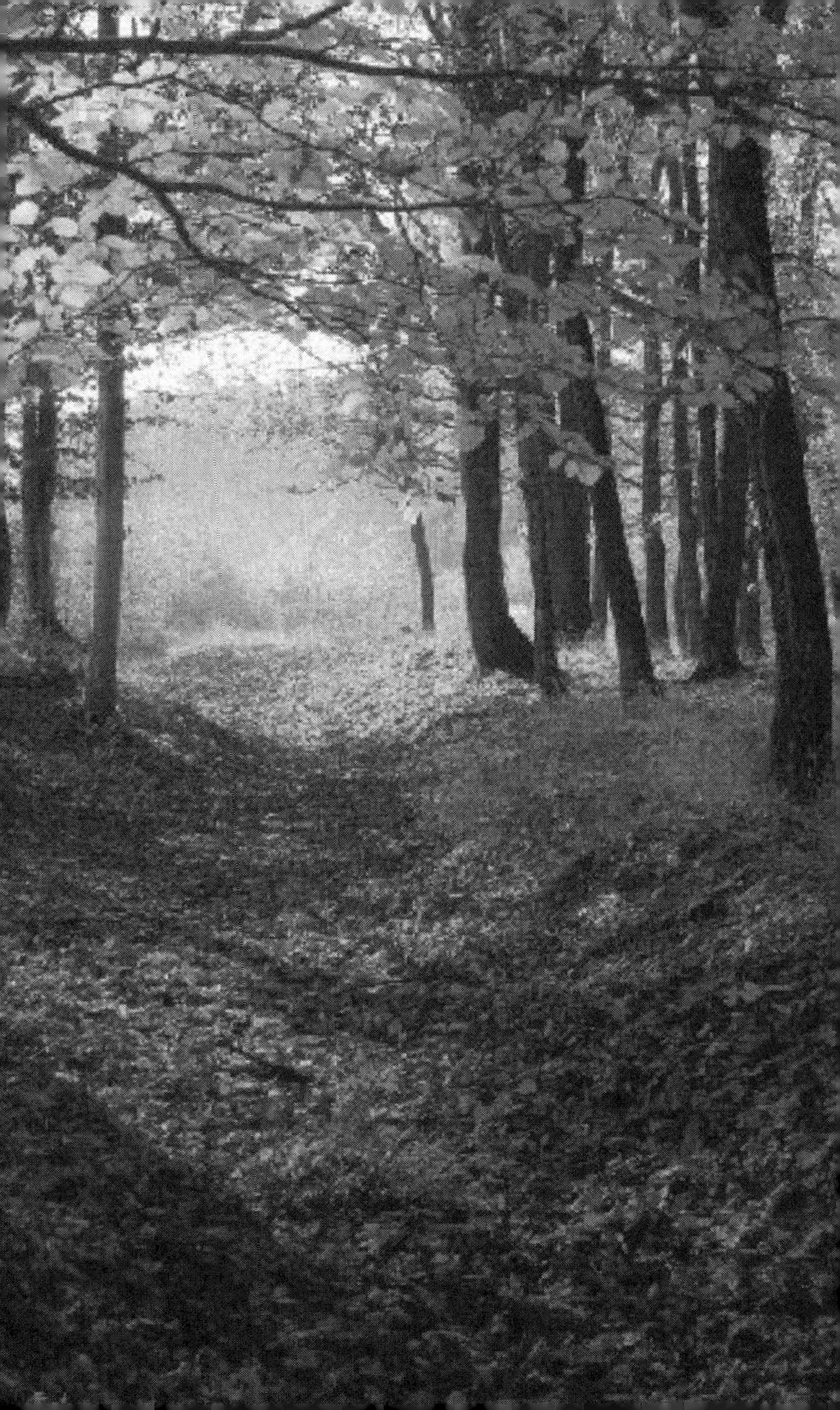

if only we could share
as much love
as the rays
of sunlight
give to us

perhaps then
the world
would be
full of peace
and harmony

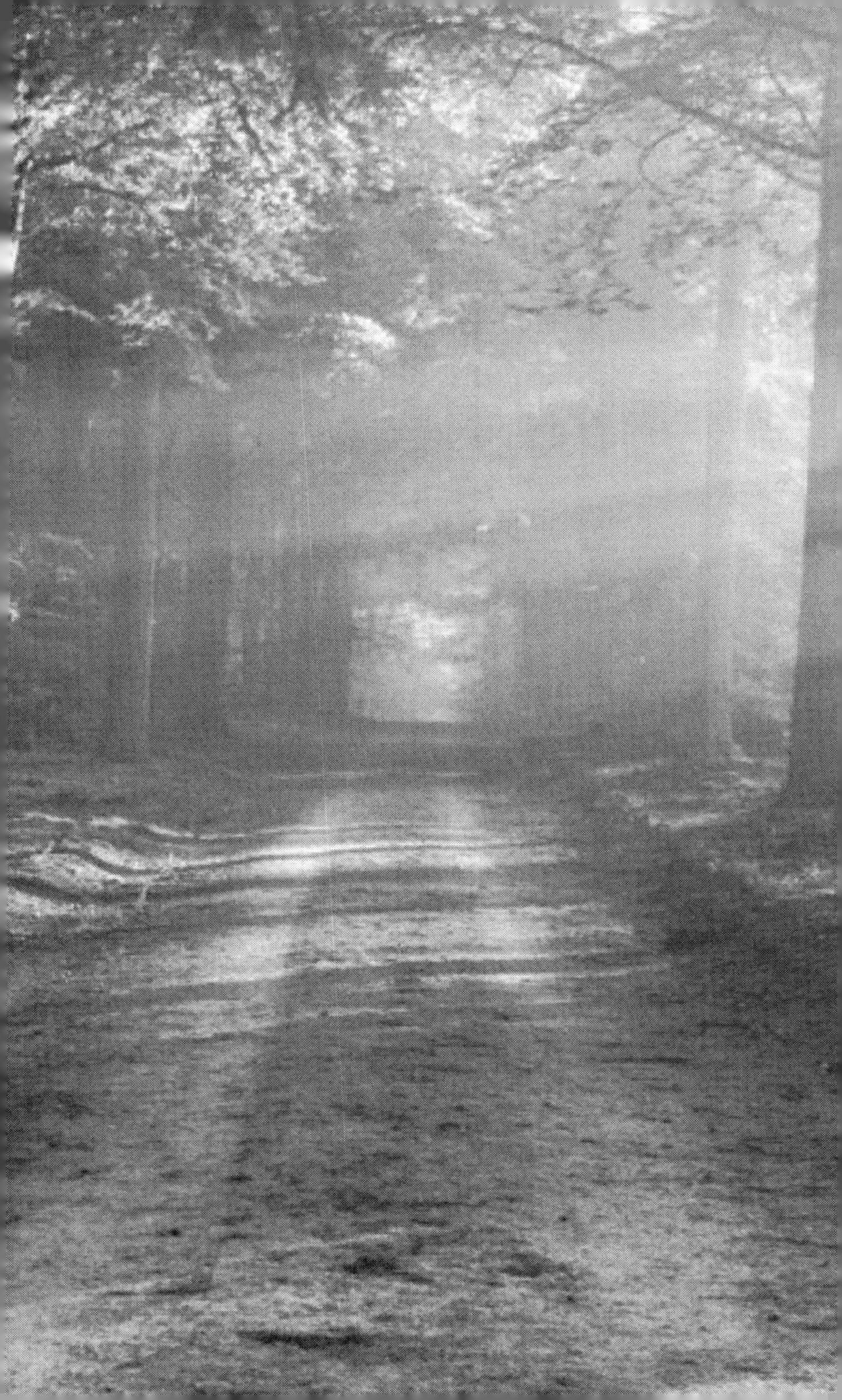

grow
like the rose

that does not try to grow
it simply does

this is the way
the universe created you
as well

you were created
to bloom
and give beauty
to the world

effortlessly
and powerfully

this is our true nature
in all its grandeur

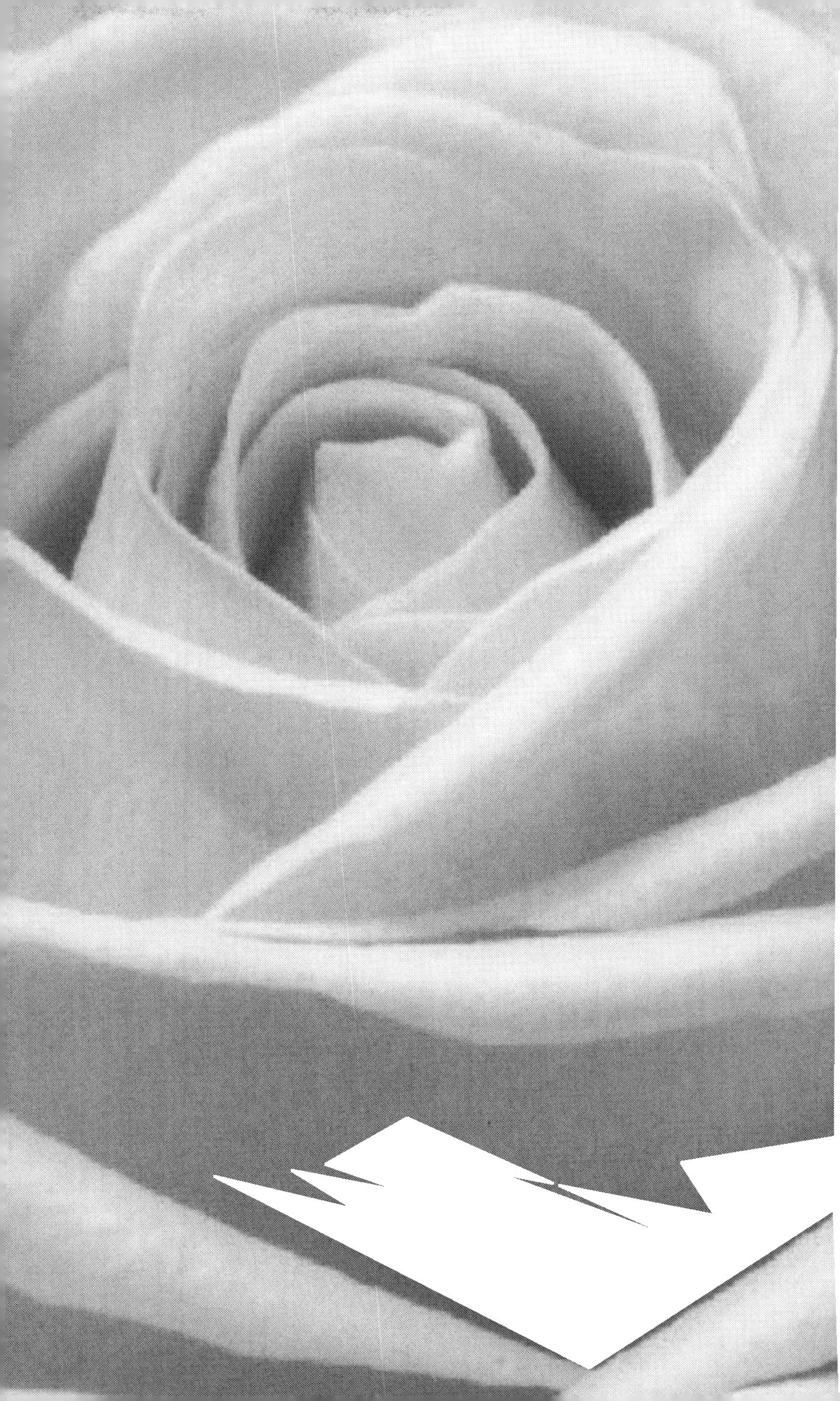

we must accept
the current moment
completely and totally
without reservation;
good and bad.

once we do so
we can tap into
the true power
of the universe

and act
in harmony with life itself
to bend existence
towards harmony and love.

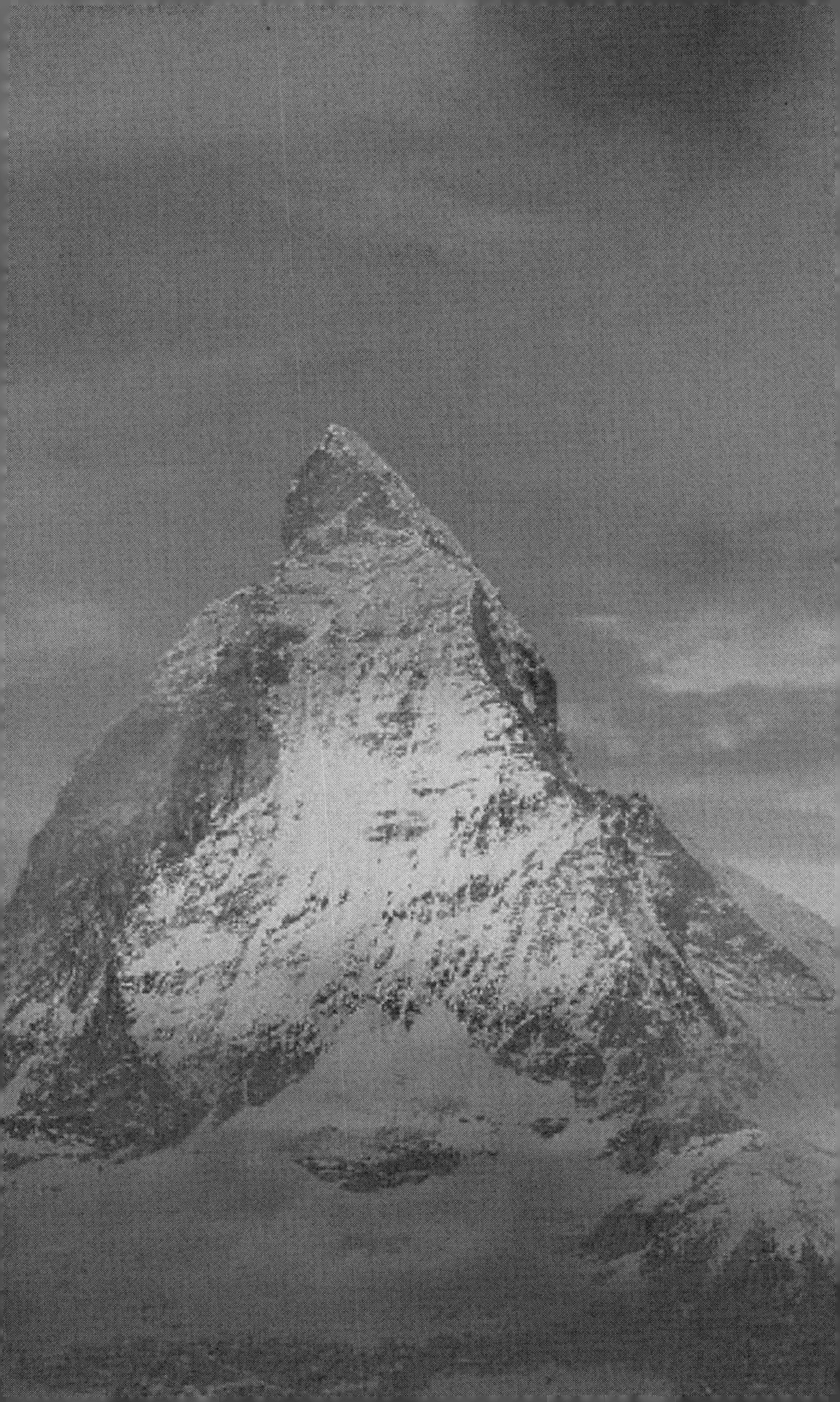

Dear Reader,

Thank you for reading my debut poetry collection. I hope that this book has helped you find peace and healing, and harmony with life.

Be well, and be loved, for the whole universe wants you to be so.

Many blessings,

Alice Harmon
Alice Harmon

Printed in Great Britain
by Amazon